THE SECOND FOUNDING

In *The Second Founding: An Introduction to the Fourteenth Amendment*, Ilan Wurman provides an illuminating introduction to the original meaning of the Fourteenth Amendment's famous provisions "due process of law," "equal protection of the laws," and the "privileges or immunities" of citizenship. He begins by exploring the antebellum legal meanings of these concepts, from Magna Carta, the Statutes of Edward III, and the Petition of Right to William Blackstone and antebellum state court cases. The book then traces how these concepts solved historical problems confronting the framers of the Fourteenth Amendment, including the comity rights of free blacks, private violence and the denial of the protection of the laws, and the notorious abridgment of freedmen's rights in the Black Codes. Wurman makes a compelling case that if the modern originalist Supreme Court were to interpret the Amendment in "the language of the law," it would lead to surprising and desirable results today.

Ilan Wurman is Associate Professor of Law at the Sandra Day O'Connor College of Law at Arizona State University, where he teaches constitutional law. He is the author of *A Debt against the Living: An Introduction to Originalism* (Cambridge University Press, 2017), and he publishes on administrative law and constitutional law in the nation's leading law journals.

The Second Founding

AN INTRODUCTION TO THE FOURTEENTH AMENDMENT

Ilan Wurman

Sandra Day O'Connor College of Law at Arizona State University

CAMBRIDGE
UNIVERSITY PRESS

CAMBRIDGE
UNIVERSITY PRESS

University Printing House, Cambridge CB2 8BS, United Kingdom

One Liberty Plaza, 20th Floor, New York, NY 10006, USA

477 Williamstown Road, Port Melbourne, VIC 3207, Australia

314–321, 3rd Floor, Plot 3, Splendor Forum, Jasola District Centre,
New Delhi – 110025, India

79 Anson Road, #06–04/06, Singapore 079906

Cambridge University Press is part of the University of Cambridge.

It furthers the University's mission by disseminating knowledge in the pursuit of
education, learning, and research at the highest international levels of excellence.

www.cambridge.org
Information on this title: www.cambridge.org/9781108843157
DOI: 10.1017/9781108914956

© Ilan Wurman 2020

First published 2020

A catalogue record for this publication is available from the British Library.

ISBN 978-1-108-84315-7 Hardback
ISBN 978-1-108-82395-1 Paperback

To the members of the Thirty-Ninth Congress;
may your work not be forgotten.

CONTENTS

ACKNOWLEDGMENTS

This is my second book. I am extremely fortunate to have an editor at Cambridge University Press, Matt Gallaway, who has now taken a chance on a young scholar not once but twice. I could not be more grateful for his faith in this project and my work.

I also owe thanks to Earl Maltz, Julian Mortenson, David Upham, and William Wiecek, who read earlier versions of the entire manuscript and some of whom disagreed with much of what it says. Engaging in good spirit with the scholars with whom one disagrees is the most important part of our profession. David Bernstein and Andy Koppelman also provided valuable feedback. I owe a special thanks to Christopher Green, who may know more about the history and drafting of the Fourteenth Amendment than any other scholar. He read my manuscript with a fine-toothed comb, pointing out several errors and corresponding with me on issues large and small. Any errors that remain are, of course, my own. I am also indebted to four anonymous reviewers whose comments helped to improve the book tremendously.

Thanks also go to Ze'ev Wurman and Chase Kassel, two of the most important nonlawyers in my life, who also read the manuscript; the reader has them to thank for improvements to the readability and accessibility of this short volume. And thanks to Jessica Kemper and Emiley Pagrabs, both first in their respective classes at the Sandra Day O'Connor College of Law at Arizona State University, for truly tremendous research assistance. Finally, thanks to Kevin Wang, a precocious undergraduate at Washington University in St. Louis, for perceptive comments and questions on an earlier draft.

But perhaps the most thanks go to the members of the Thirty-Ninth Congress, those framers of the Fourteenth Amendment: they gave us an improvement to the eternal firmament of the U.S. Constitution, without which the Constitution would have had to be abandoned long ago. We today are truly indebted to their achievement.

NOTE ON THE COVER

The image, published in *Harper's Weekly* in 1867, illustrates the first time the newly freed men voted after the abolition of slavery. Although the Fourteenth Amendment did not guarantee their right to vote—only the Fifteenth Amendment, ratified in 1870, would so guarantee—these newly freed men were instrumental in electing and serving as delegates to new state constitutional conventions under the reconstruction governments in the South. The new state legislatures constituted under these new constitutions would supply the final votes needed for ratification of the Fourteenth Amendment.

INTRODUCTION

"All persons born or naturalized in the United States, and subject to the jurisdiction thereof, are citizens of the United States and of the State wherein they reside. No State shall make or enforce any law which shall abridge the privileges or immunities of citizens of the United States; nor shall any State deprive any person of life, liberty, or property, without due process of law; nor deny to any person within its jurisdiction the equal protection of the laws."

U.S. Constitution, amend. XIV.

The standard public debate over the Fourteenth Amendment goes something like this. Critics of the Supreme Court's interpretations of the Fourteenth Amendment over the last several decades believe that the Court has used the Amendment's provisions for "due process of law" and "equal protection of the laws" as open-ended vehicles for judicial policymaking, whether on abortion or gay marriage or a host of other issues. Indeed, it is difficult for someone sympathetic to the result in the 2015 gay marriage case *Obergefell v. Hodges*[1] to read the Court's opinion and get the feeling that what the Court is doing is *law*. The case was decided under the rather nebulous concept "substantive due process": the idea that the Fourteenth Amendment's injunction that no person shall be deprived of life, liberty, or property without due process of law is not merely about process, as its terms might suggest, but also about "substance" – namely, that the clause protects unwritten, unenumerated fundamental rights or prohibits arbitrary and oppressive legislation.

The majority of the Supreme Court also seemed to believe that it was up to them to decide over time how those unenumerated, fundamental rights ought to evolve. Although "[h]istory and tradition guide

1

and discipline this inquiry," they "do not set its outer boundaries." "The identification" of fundamental rights, Justice Kennedy wrote in *Obergefell* – not only their protection, but also the actual determination of what those rights are in the first place – "is an enduring part of the judicial duty to interpret the Constitution." What rights the Constitution insulates from democratic action cannot be "reduced to any formula," but rather courts must "exercise reasoned judgment in identifying interests of the person so fundamental that the State must accord them its respect." The courts' process is "guided" by the considerations relevant to the analysis of "other constitutional provisions that set forth broad principles rather than specific requirements." The people, Justice Kennedy wrote, "entrusted to future generations a charter protecting the right of all persons to enjoy liberty as *we learn its meaning*" – by which he meant, of course, as the Court decides its meaning.[2]

Justice Kennedy's opinion echoes one of the most influential constitutional law scholars of the last century, John Hart Ely, who wrote in his famous *Democracy and Distrust* that the Fourteenth Amendment was a broad and open-ended delegation of power to future constitutional decisionmakers.[3] Ely would have disagreed with Justice Kennedy on substantive due process: Ely was quite explicit that due process of law was indeed historically about process.[4] Nevertheless, Ely argued that the privileges or immunities clause and the equal protection clause were equally broad invitations to future courts to protect new rights. For example, the privileges or immunities clause "was a delegation to future constitutional decision-makers to protect certain rights that the document neither lists, at least not exhaustively, nor even in any specific way gives directions for finding."[5] The content of the equal protection clause, Ely wrote, "will not be found anywhere in its terms or in the ruminations of its writers," but the clause nevertheless serves as "a rather sweeping mandate to judge of the validity of governmental choices."[6]

Simply put, according to Ely, the Fourteenth Amendment "contains provisions that are difficult to read responsibly as anything other than quite broad invitations to import into the constitutional decision process considerations that will not be found in the language of the amendment or the debates that led up to it."[7] Justice Cardozo echoed this sentiment when he spoke of the Constitution's "great generalities," whose "content and . . . significance . . . vary from age to age."[8] In light of holdings and comments such as these, critics see the Fourteenth Amendment as interpreted by the modern Supreme Court and advocated by academics as a vehicle for unbounded, undemocratic judicial lawmaking.

However, proponents of this broad and open-ended approach to the Amendment – and proponents of the notion of "living constitutionalism" more generally – consider the alternative unthinkable. Reverting to the "original meaning" of the Fourteenth Amendment would mean "excluding" women, gay Americans, and other minorities from the Amendment's protections. It is a common belief, for example, that originalism cannot support the result in *Brown v. Board of Education*,[9] the seminal 1954 decision requiring the desegregation of public schools. Eric Segall, a prominent nonoriginalist law professor, wrote in *Vox* in 2017 just before the confirmation hearings of Justice Neil Gorsuch that "*Brown v. Board of Education*, one of the most important cases of the 20th century, would have turned out the other way if the justices had accepted originalist principles."[10] He described the originalist attempts to justify *Brown* as "embarrassing."

Indeed, at least some originalist alternatives would be quite hard to swallow. In dissent in *Obergefell*, Justice Antonin Scalia wrote that "[w]hen the Fourteenth Amendment was ratified . . . it is unquestionable that the People who ratified that provision did not understand it to prohibit a practice [the sanctioning of marriage between only a man and a woman] that remained both universal and uncontroversial in the years after ratification."[11] This, to Justice Scalia, should have ended the matter. But can that really be the answer? Are we bound to what people in 1868 would have understood about an issue to which no one at the time had put any thought? Are we consigned to interpreting the Fourteenth Amendment *either* as a broad and open-ended invitation to future judges to decide what a democratic people should not be able to do through self-government *or* as a narrow requirement for judges to strike down only those practices that would have been thought unconstitutional in 1868?

It turns out that neither approach does justice to the Fourteenth Amendment and its authors. The provisions they wrote were neither so broad nor so narrow. Each provision of the Amendment's first section deploys a legal concept with a rich history in antebellum law or legal theory – legal concepts that, when faithfully applied, lead to both surprising and desirable results in the modern day. For example, it is astonishingly easy to defend *Brown* and desegregation on the original meaning of the privileges or immunities clause, which provides that "[n]o State shall make or enforce any law which shall abridge the privileges or immunities of citizens of the United States." It is also possible, although not quite as easy, to arrive at the result in *Obergefell,* thereby guaranteeing the right to same-sex marriage under this clause. Whether or not the privileges or immunities clause necessarily justifies that decision, at least if the Court had justified the decision on the basis of that clause it would have appeared to all participants in the debate that the Court was making an honest attempt at doing "law" and less that it was simply making it up.

In short, the argument presented here is that the Fourteenth Amendment was written with legal terms of art – terms that were sufficiently capacious to apply to new and important contexts, but not so capacious as to be open-ended invitations to judges to import their own extratextual values into the Constitution. This short book seeks to introduce the reader to the meaning and history of the Fourteenth Amendment's three key provisions in its famous first section – the privileges or immunities clause, the due process clause, and the equal protection clause – as well as that section's grant of birthright citizenship.

My attempt here is similar to that in my book *A Debt against the Living: An Introduction to Originalism,*[12] which sought to introduce originalism to a broader audience by uncovering and elaborating the general findings and conclusions of originalist scholars over the last few decades. Very much as with that book, however, this book is not quite a "neutral" introduction. It explains the debates, provides the best arguments of the various sides, and then offers its own position. Although the book – and particularly its methodology – will certainly be of interest to scholars, my overarching objective has been to write a short book that is introductory and accessible to any and all interested in the original meaning of the Fourteenth Amendment.

METHODOLOGY

Another word must be said about methodology. Most other books written on the original meaning of the Fourteenth Amendment focus on the debates in Congress[13] or the general antislavery and political history of the antebellum period.[14] Although legislative history can surely be consulted profitably, doing so suffers acutely from the more general problem of using legislative history to interpret statutes. In the first place, most of the framers of the Fourteenth Amendment did not think about the various applications with which constitutional litigation is concerned today and did not even think very carefully about the specific applications in their own time.[15]

Second, picking and choosing statements from the legislative history for support is, in the oft-repeated words of Judge Harold Leventhal, rather like "looking over a crowd and picking out your friends."[16] Incorporation is a classic example. Most proponents of the incorporation of the Bill of Rights against the states cite a single statement by Senator Howard when introducing the Amendment to the Senate, as well as a few stray and ambiguous statements by Representative Bingham, who was the principal author of the Amendment's first section.[17] More generally, as one correspondent put it when reporting on Congress's reconstruction efforts in 1866: "It is a Babel of opinion here – a political chaos. No two prominent men think alike."[18] A casual perusal of the congressional debates in 1866 confirms this observation.[19]

A different school of thought abandons the legislative history altogether and insists on the open-ended nature of the Fourteenth Amendment's provisions. John Hart Ely was only one of the more prominent of such scholars.[20] Those who focus on the general anti-slavery political history of the Amendment also claim it was a "vague charter for the future," not designed "to provide judges with a determinative text," but rather, for example, "to reaffirm the lay public's longstanding rhetorical commitment to general principles of equality, individual rights, and local self-rule."[21] Eric Foner, in his recent short treatment of the Reconstruction Amendments, asserts that "[t]he crucial first section of the Fourteenth Amendment is written in the language of general principles – due process, equal protection, privileges or immunities of citizenship – that cry out for further elaboration, making it inevitable that their specific applications would be the subject of never-ending contention."[22] These historians further ignore that abolitionists may have had idiosyncratic and erroneous views of the Constitution in the antebellum period, that the public did not necessarily share their understanding of the Reconstruction Amendments, and that the language they used in those Amendments often did not capture what some of them may have wanted or intended.[23]

In short, neither prevailing approach, it seems to me, is satisfactory. An approach that turns on legislative history is likely to be too narrow and too amenable to manipulation; an approach that turns on "broad invitations" to import extratextual values into the Amendment is likely to be too broad and similarly amenable to manipulation.

The method of this book, in contrast, is to uncover the original legal meanings of the Amendment's key provisions in antebellum law and to show how these legal concepts, when deployed in the Fourteenth Amendment, solved the general historical problems known to both the framers and the public of the era. As far as I am aware, this is only the second book to attempt an introduction to the Fourteenth Amendment in terms of the language of the law as opposed to using the legislative history or broader antislavery constitutional understandings.[24] I do not claim that the framers of the Amendment necessarily understood the full import of the legal language they deployed. What I claim is that they did use legal language, and both Representative Bingham and Senator Howard may have even expected judges to interpret the Amendment's language legally.[25]

In this book, I shall highlight the three principal constitutional questions or problems in this period relevant to the Fourteenth Amendment: whether free blacks* were "citizens of the United States" within the meaning of the Constitution, such that they were entitled to rights under the comity clause in Article IV (declaring that

---

* In using this term here and elsewhere, I seek to be faithful to the way in which the historical sources distinguish between enslaved and free African Americans and to the historical debate, definitively resolved by the Fourteenth Amendment itself, over whether newly freed black people were "Americans" in the sense of having citizenship.

"[t]he Citizens of each State shall be entitled to all Privileges and Immunities of Citizens in the several States"); the widespread private violence against blacks, abolitionists, and later Unionists; and finally the enactment of the Black Codes in the South after the Civil War that systematically denied the newly freed men and women the same basic rights that white citizens enjoyed.

The Thirty-Ninth Congress in 1866–67 tried to rectify all of these abridgments, denials, and deprivations with three pieces of legislation: the Civil Rights Act of 1866, the Privileges and Immunities Bill, and the Second Freedmen's Bureau Act. Each of these Acts had known constitutional infirmities, and it has often been observed that the Fourteenth Amendment was intended at least to give a constitutional basis for the Civil Rights Act of 1866.[26] This book aims to show that the Fourteenth Amendment deployed the well-established legal concepts "privileges and immunities," "due process of law," and "protection of the laws," as well as birthright citizenship, to constitutionalize these various pieces of legislation. These Acts, as well as the Fourteenth Amendment itself, were intended to solve the question of the citizenship status of free blacks and their interstate comity rights, the abridgment of the intrastate rights of the newly freed men and women in the Black Codes, and the known problem of private violence and inadequate protection of the laws in the South and elsewhere.

The meaning and intended legal effect of the Amendment's provisions, in other words, become clear – perhaps even inescapable – when we consider the legal concepts the Amendment employed and the specific historical problems the Amendment was intended to solve. And this meaning is clear with minimal resort to the less reliable legislative debates in Congress. To be sure, we must resort to at least some *general* legislative history. For example, we shall refer to the fact that at least eighteen members of Congress stated that the purpose of the Fourteenth Amendment was to constitutionalize the Civil Rights Act (compared to only one or perhaps two who said anything about incorporating the Bill of Rights).

One might object to this distinction between relying on known general historical problems on the one hand and relying on specific statements from the legislative debates on the other. Yet this is exactly

the distinction between relying on "purpose" in statutory interpretation, which originalists tend to support, and relying on "legislative
history," which they do not. (That is not to say, of course, that one
could not support, or oppose, the use of both.) And it is the distinction
that the Supreme Court adopted in interpreting the Fourteenth
Amendment over 100 years ago:

> A constitutional amendment must be agreed to, not only by
> Senators and Representatives, but it must be ratified by the legis-
> latures, or by conventions, in three fourths of the states before such
> amendment can take effect. The safe way is to read its language in
> connection with the known condition of affairs out of which the
> occasion for its adoption may have arisen, and then to construe it, if
> there be therein any doubtful expressions, in a way, so far as is
> reasonably possible, to forward the known purpose or object for
> which the amendment was adopted.[27]

In short, an approach that focuses on the known legal concepts, the
known historical problems, and only the most general legislative history
to show awareness that the legal concepts were deployed to solve those
historical problems is a far more reliable approach than one that
plumbs the legislative debates for friendly but stray comments. Not
only is this approach more reliable, but also the meaning and intended
effect of the Fourteenth Amendment that emerge from this analysis
chart a satisfying course between the overly broad approach of the
modern Supreme Court and what opponents of "originalism" fear
will be an overly rigid and wooden approach.[28]

THE ROADMAP

The roadmap and argument are as follows. The book is divided into
three parts, covering the antebellum legal concepts, the historical problems that the Fourteenth Amendment was designed to address, and
how the Amendment would apply today to key historical cases and
a few salient modern ones.

Part I, comprising the first three chapters, explores the antebellum legal concepts "due process of law," "protection of the laws,"

and "privileges and immunities of citizenship." In Chapter 1, we shall see that due process of law meant only that no person could be deprived of life, liberty, or property except according to preexisting, established laws, and that violations of those laws had to be adjudicated according to a certain minimum of common-law judicial procedures. This means that there was no "substantive" component to due process in antebellum law that protected fundamental rights, with the exception of one or two notorious cases. When antebellum authors wrote that the clause protected against "arbitrary" government acts, they did not mean that a court could review legislative acts to see if they were arbitrary on the merits. They meant arbitrary in the sense in which John Locke used the term: an *arbitrary* government act was an act made extemporaneously, contrary to promulgated, standing laws. The chapter will conclude by briefly surveying the antislavery constitutional theorists. It is often believed that they advanced a vision of substantive due process; this chapter will argue that their vision was consistent with the procedural understanding.

Chapter 2 will explore the use of the phrase "protection of the laws" in antebellum legal theory and demonstrate that it referred to specific kinds of laws: those that protected one's existing rights in life, liberty, or property. These were the laws that protected against physical harms and threats to liberty, as well as threats to and intrusions on private property, from other private citizens. This was the "flip side" of due process: due process of law established the rules by which the government could deprive a person of life, liberty, or property, and the protection of the laws was the protection the government had to provide against private interference with these rights. We shall here discuss the political theory of the American Founding to show that a government had to provide this protection for it to be legitimate and worthy of obedience.

Chapter 3 will turn to the antebellum legal concept of the privileges and immunities of citizenship. It will show how privileges and immunities clauses in antebellum law, including in treaties, state constitutions, and the original U.S. Constitution, were generally nondiscrimination provisions. The comity clause of Article IV of the U.S. Constitution, for example, meant that whatever privileges and immunities a state *chose* to grant its citizens as a part of their citizenship, it had to grant those same privileges and immunities (with certain obvious or at least inherent exceptions) to citizens of other states sojourning within its jurisdiction.

Part II – comprising the next three chapters – will show that the problem the Fourteenth Amendment's authors sought to solve was the systematic exclusion of blacks from the benefits of all of these privileges and rights. Chapter 4 will describe the three fundamental problems that the Fourteenth Amendment would eventually address: whether free blacks were "citizens of the United States" such that they were entitled to the privileges and immunities of other citizens under the comity clause when engaging in interstate travel; the problem of private violence against blacks, abolitionists, and later Unionists, and the concomitant denial of the protection of the laws; and, finally, the systematic exclusion of the newly freed people from the civil rights enjoyed by white citizens under the infamous postbellum Black Codes.

Chapter 5 will go through the legislation of the Thirty-Ninth Congress: the Civil Rights Act of 1866, the Privileges and Immunities Bill, and the Second Freedmen's Bureau Act. It demonstrates that these Acts would have directly addressed these three problems of interstate comity rights, private violence and the denial of the protection of the laws, and the abridgment of civil rights in the Black Codes. It will further demonstrate that the constitutional basis for these Acts was generally contested and that the Fourteenth Amendment constitutionalized them by deploying birthright citizenship and the antebellum legal concepts discussed in Part I.

The very first sentence of the Amendment declared that the now-freed blacks were "citizens of the United States," therefore settling once and for all their rights to interstate comity (and other constitutional rights). The prohibition on denying the protection of the laws, and the corollary prohibition on depriving any person of life, liberty, or property without due process of law, would allow Congress and the federal courts to step in to prevent private violence. And the privileges or immunities clause – declaring that no state shall make or enforce any law which shall abridge the privileges or immunities of citizens of the United States – did for *intra*state discrimination what the comity clause did for *inter*state discrimination: it abolished the Black Codes and required equality in civil rights.

The privileges or immunities clause, in other words, was almost certainly an antidiscrimination provision. It likely was not intended to guarantee any fundamental rights at all, but rather to ensure fundamental equality in the provision of any civil rights a state accorded its citizens. Chapter 6 will take a deeper dive into the evidence about and debate over the privileges or immunities clause. It will tack away from our affirmative story and show why the principal alternatives to this antidiscrimination reading are likely incorrect.

Chapter 7 wraps up the book as Part III. It gives a quick overview of the history of the interpretation of the Fourteenth Amendment: how the Supreme Court effectively wrote the privileges or immunities clause out of the Amendment and had to warp the meanings of the equal protection and due process clauses to fix its own mistake. This chapter will then show how *Brown v. Board of Education* is an easy case under the privileges or immunities clause. *Obergefell v. Hodges* is also an easier case under privileges or immunities than under substantive due process (or under equal protection), although it is by no means foolproof. This chapter will also show how the clause likely prohibits extreme economic favoritism, but probably does not prohibit the mine run of modern economic legislation. It will suggest that prohibitions on discrimination in public accommodations are likely constitutional. It will end with some brief comments on the enforcement power of the Fourteenth Amendment's fifth section.

In each of the chapters to come, we will see that originalists disagree among themselves about the various issues. I hope I have adequately surveyed the various positions, and the reader may, of course, consult the notes for further reading along interesting lines of inquiry. Yet the historical concepts and problems that this book aims to uncover and convey make a compelling case for the vision of the Fourteenth Amendment presented here – a vision whose contemporary appeal is as compelling as its historical one.

PART I

Antebellum Law

1 DUE PROCESS OF LAW

"No free man shall be taken, imprisoned, disseised, outlawed, banished, or in any way destroyed . . . except by the lawful judgment of his peers or by the law of the land."

Magna Carta, ch. 39, 1215

Two concepts form the core of modern Fourteenth Amendment jurisprudence. The first, equal protection, is today interpreted to require general equality and nondiscrimination in a state's laws. The other, "substantive due process," guarantees both written and unwritten fundamental rights against any infringement whatsoever by a state. It is through "substantive due process" that the Supreme Court has incorporated the Bill of Rights against the states. And it is through this concept that the Court in the early twentieth century protected economic contract rights from state legislation in cases such as *Lochner v. New York*,[1] which invalidated as arbitrary a state law limiting the number of hours bakers could work in a day. Substantive due process is the concept that the Court has used to justify a constitutional right to abortion, contraceptives, sexual intimacy, and same-sex marriage.

Substantive due process may be a contradiction in terms. In the words of John Hart Ely, it is "sort of like 'green pastel redness.' "[2] And yet some version of this concept has defenders even among originalists, although they tend to reject the substantive due process label. These originalists, like Randy Barnett and Evan Bernick, argue that an originalist interpretation of the two federal due process clauses[3] that takes into account their letter and "spirit" requires courts to examine state legislative acts to determine whether they were enacted in a good-faith pursuit of the legitimate ends of free government.[4] The federal due process clause and its state constitutional equivalents, they argue, historically provided "substantive protection from arbitrary power."[5] Therefore courts must develop some kind of "police powers" doctrine that takes into account the legitimate ends of government and ensures that state legislatures (and the federal government) enact laws only in pursuance of those legitimate powers.[6]

Kurt Lash, another originalist scholar, has similarly claimed that the framers of the Fourteenth Amendment understood due process to protect unwritten fundamental rights, including the right to contract and to acquire and possess property.[7] David Bernstein has argued that "the idea that the guarantee of 'due process of law' regulates the substance of legislation ... arose from the long-standing Anglo-American principle that the government has inherently limited powers" and from "long-standing American intellectual traditions that held that the government had no authority to enforce arbitrary 'class legislation' or to violate the fundamental natural rights of the American people."[8] Several other originalists have made similar claims.[9]

The best originalist evidence, however, goes against these claims. This chapter shows that due process of law was indeed about "process." Since its inception in Magna Carta, due process of law meant only that no person could be deprived of life, liberty, or property except according to preexisting, standing laws, and violations of those laws had to be adjudicated according to certain common-law or statutorily established judicial procedures. In other words, there had to be a *law* that was violated before a person could be deprived of life, liberty, or property: neither the legislature nor the executive could deprive someone of these rights for having committed acts that violated no preexisting law. And there had to be adequate *procedure*: a violation of existing law generally had to be adjudicated by a common-law court according to common-law procedures or by the lawful judgment of one's peers.[10]

DUE PROCESS ACCORDING TO ESTABLISHED LAW

Americans inherited the concept of due process of law from their English forebears. We can track the development of the concept through four sets of constitutional struggles or legal texts: Magna Carta in 1215, the various Statutes of Edward III in the 1300s, the Petition of Right in 1628, and finally William Blackstone's *Commentaries on the Laws of England*, which were published in 1765 and heavily influenced the American Founders.

Magna Carta

The origin of the legal concept "due process of law" is usually traced to Chapter 39 of Magna Carta (Chapter 29 in later versions), which the English barons compelled King John to sign in 1215. In this famous clause, the Great Charter provided that "[n]o free man shall be taken, imprisoned, disseised, outlawed, banished, or in any way destroyed ... except by the lawful judgment of his peers or by the law of the land."[11] The connection to deprivations of life, liberty, and property is clear: "disseised" is the Anglo-French term for being deprived of property, and the other terms in Magna Carta relate to imprisonment, banishment, death, and other physical harm.

The question is, under what conditions could the state legitimately deprive someone of life, liberty, or property? A "lawful" judgment of peers seems to imply both a certain kind of process and preexisting law. A deprivation can occur only after a trial by jury (a particular process), and that judgment also had to be "lawful," which seems to have meant according to known laws.[12] A deprivation "by the law of the land" also required established laws and known processes. Whatever this law of the land entailed, whether custom or common law or statute law, the idea was that such laws were known and established. The king could not, merely by extemporaneous decree, deprive a subject of life, liberty, or property. And whatever processes existed other than trial by jury, for example, in disputes over government property,[13] such processes would have been *known* to the law of the land.

Statutes of Edward III

The substance of these requirements was soon described as "due process of law." At least three statutes enacted in the time of King Edward III – in 1351, 1354, and 1368 – reiterated the grand injunction of Magna Carta. (One suspects the Great Charter was breached at least as much as it was honored.) The 1351 statute reminded the king that:

> Whereas it is contained in the Great Charter . . . that none shall be imprisoned nor put out of his Freehold, nor of his Franchises nor free Custom, unless it be by the Law of the Land, . . . henceforth none shall be taken by Petition or Suggestion made to our Lord the King, or to his Council, unless it be by Indictment or Presentment of good and lawful People of the same neighbourhood where such Deeds be done, in due Manner, or by Process made by Writ original at the Common Law; nor that none be out of his Franchises, nor of his Freeholds, unless he be duly brought into answer, and forejudged of the same by the Course of the Law.[14]

This statute did not use the "due process of law" formulation, but it reiterated the "law of the land" requirement: no one shall be deprived of liberty merely by a petition to or decree of the king. Only a few routes were available to work a deprivation of someone's rights. First, the statute allowed for an "indictment" or "presentment" by a grand jury "in due manner." Second, it allowed for "process made by writ original at the common law." Third, a subject could be put "out of" franchises and freeholds only if "he be duly brought into answer, and forejudged of the same by the Course of the Law."

The substance of these requirements appears to be, again, twofold: First, a certain *process* was required, such as a grand jury and trial or some other process according to the known and established common law writs; and, second, there must have been some law establishing the underlying offense. This can be understood especially from the requirement of process by common-law writs. These writs were very specific and precisely defined the obligations of subjects to one another.[15] Thus the "process" by common-law writ, the "course of the law," and the "law of the land" did not merely require a certain process, but also guaranteed the benefit of known and established rules of conduct.

The phrase "due process of law" first appears in the 1354 statute. That statute provided "[t]hat no Man of what Estate or Condition that he be, shall be put out of Land or Tenement, nor taken, nor imprisoned, nor disinherited, nor put to Death, without being brought in

Answer by due Process of the Law."[16] It seems quite apparent that "due process of the law" here entails the same requirements as those of the 1351 statute. No one shall be deprived of life by being put to death, liberty by being imprisoned, or property by being put out of land, tenement, or inheritance, except by the "process" of the law – the same "course of law," the same common-law writs, the same lawful judgment of one's peers described in the 1351 statute and in Magna Carta.

Then, in 1368, Parliament's third statute explicitly equated due process of law with common-law writs and the law of the land. In this statute, Parliament (and the king) "assented and accorded, for the good Governance of the Commons, that no Man be put to answer without Presentment before Justices, or Matter of Record, or by due Process and Writ original, according to the old Law of the Land."[17] Hence "due process" is the process "according to the old law of the land."

Summing up these early statutes, it would appear that due process of law meant that no person could be deprived of life, liberty, or property without the benefit of *established law* – that is, law establishing the underlying criminal or civil offense: the common-law writs or the "law of the land." And if a violation occurred, the subject was entitled to the procedural protection of the common law, which for certain offenses required a grand jury indictment and trial by jury. At least at this early juncture, we can say with some confidence that due process did not entail a substantive component; it did not prohibit Parliament from establishing laws that were unreasonable in substance. There simply had to *be* law that was violated before someone could be deprived of the fundamental natural rights to life, liberty, and property.

Petition of Right

This concept of due process of law remained stable over the next centuries, even as it was routinely breached. One of the most critical subsequent encounters with due process in constitutional history is in the Petition of Right of 1628, submitted to the king a decade or so before the English Civil War would begin in earnest. Charles I was in great need of money, and yet existing statutes prohibited him from compelling his subjects to give the Crown payments without parliamentary consent. Charles tried rather too cleverly to get around these restrictions by compelling his subjects to *lend* him the money instead; he required his subjects to pay a "forced loan."[18] There was a general resistance to this policy, leading to widespread arrests.[19] In a case of particular importance, "The Trial of the Five Knights" or the *Five Knights' Case*, five imprisoned gentlemen sought a writ of habeas corpus to compel the king to state the cause for their imprisonment. The king's courts (there was as of yet no separation of executive and judicial functions) held that the king was not required to state any cause. This became a *cause célèbre* and concentrated the public mind on the king's transgressions.[20]

When Parliament had to be called in 1628, the king thought it expedient to release seventy-six subjects whom he had imprisoned for failure to pay the forced loan.[21] Twenty-seven of these men were sent to the new Parliament, and they immediately attacked the king's policy of "arbitrary taxation and arbitrary imprisonment."[22] They also immediately connected the king's policies with a transgression of Magna Carta. "I shall be very glad," said one member, "to see that good old decrepit law of Magna Charta, which hath been kept so long and lien bedrid, as it were – I shall be glad to see it walk abroad again, with new vigour and lustre."[23]

The Commons and Lords presented a petition to the king, the Petition of Right. It is worth quoting at some length, because it seems to establish beyond doubt the two requirements of due process of law. The first paragraph deals with the historic right to be taxed only with Parliament's consent. The second complains that, as a result of the forced loan policy, the king's subjects have been "bound to make Appearance and give Attendance before Your Privy Council and in other Places; and others of them have been therefore imprisoned, confined, and sundry other Ways molested and disquieted; and divers other Charges have been laid and levied upon Your People" by the mere "Command or Direction from Your Majesty, or Your Privy Council, *against the Laws and Free Customs of the Realm.*" Immediately, we see how arbitrary imprisonment or deprivations by mere "command" of the king, without the backing of established laws, is contrary to the requirements of due process of law.[24]

The next two paragraphs make this clear, reminding the king of the requirements of Magna Carta and the Statutes of Edward III:

> And where also by the statute called *The Great Charter of the Liberties of England*, it is declared and enacted, That no Freeman may be taken or imprisoned, or be disseised of his Freehold or Liberties, or his Free Customs, or be outlawed or exiled, or in any manner destroyed, but by the lawful Judgment of his Peers, or by the Law of the Land. ... And in the Eight and twentieth Year of the Reign of King *Edward* the Third it was declared and enacted by Authority of Parliament, That no Man of what Estate or Condition that he be, should be put out of his Land or Tenements, nor taken, nor imprisoned, nor disherited, nor put to Death, without being brought to answer by due Process of Law.

The Petition contends that, despite these statutory protections, "divers of Your Subjects have of late been imprisoned without any Cause shewed." When the five knights sued for a writ of habeas corpus, "no Cause was certified," and the knights were "returned back to several Prisons, without being charged with any Thing to which they might *make Answer according to the Law*."[25] The tenor of this portion of the Petition of Right is unmistakable: due process of law is denied where subjects are deprived of life, liberty, or property on the basis of no known and established rule of law. A subject can be deprived of these critical rights only *according to law* – according to established rules of conduct.

The Petition of Right further reveals that due process also required certain procedures to determine that a violation of law had occurred. The Petition separately referred to the Great Charter and to the statute of Edward III's twenty-fifth year, which – together with other laws and statutes of the realm – provided that "no Man ought to be *adjudged* to Death but *by the Laws established* in this Your Realm, either by the Customs of the same Realm, or by Acts of Parliament." More specifically, "no Offender of what Kind soever is exempted from the *Proceedings to be used, and Punishments to be inflicted by the Laws and Statutes of this Your Realm*." Charles I had been violating these procedural requirements of the established laws by using instead the "summary Course" of martial law, by which some subjects had been "put to

Death, when and where, if by the Laws and Statutes of the Land they had deserved Death, *by the same Laws and Statutes also they might, and by no other ought to have been judged and executed.*"[26]

In short, the Petition of Right of 1628 reveals even more explicitly what one could already discern from Magna Carta and the Statutes of Edward III: due process of law permitted deprivations of right only according to *known laws* and according to the law's *known procedures*.

Blackstone's *Commentaries*

William Blackstone's *Commentaries on the Laws of England*, published in 1765 and hugely influential on the American Founders, confirms the historical understanding in his chapter on the "absolute rights of individuals." Blackstone wrote that the natural rights of the subject are threefold: "the right of personal security, the right of personal liberty; and the right of private property."[27] The right to life is so important, wrote Blackstone, that "the constitution is an utter stranger to any arbitrary power of killing or maiming the subject without the express warrant of law."[28] Blackstone quoted for this proposition Chapter 39/29 of Magna Carta, as well as two of the Statutes of Edward III.[29] Due process of law, in other words, meant that there must be "express warrant in law" before there could be a sentence of death.

Blackstone next turned to liberty. He explained that no subject could be imprisoned or restrained "unless by due course of law" and that this right to personal liberty "cannot ever be abridged at the mere discretion of the magistrate, without the explicit permission of the laws."[30] Here, again, Blackstone cited "the language of the great charter ... that no freeman shall be taken or imprisoned, but by the lawful judgment of his equals, or by the law of the land."[31] Due process of law and the law of the land, in other words, required "the explicit permission of the laws" to work a deprivation of liberty. As for the right to property, "which consists in the free use, enjoyment, and disposal of all his acquisitions, without any control or diminution, save only by the laws of the land," here, too, Blackstone wrote that Magna Carta and the statute law of England are "extremely watchful in ascertaining and protecting this right."[32]

The requirement that there be "express warrant in law" or the "explicit permission of the laws" takes on additional significance in light of Blackstone's earlier definition of law. In a chapter on the characteristics of law, Blackstone wrote that laws properly so called are rules "*prescribed*" – that is, they must be made known to the people: "[A] bare resolution, confined in the breast of the legislator, without manifesting itself by some external sign, can never be properly a law."[33] To properly be a law, it is "requisite that this resolution be notified to the people who are to obey it" in a "public and perspicuous manner."[34] For this reason, laws must also "commence *in futuro*, and be notified before their commencement."[35] In other words, a mere command declaring that a subject had committed some unlawful act where the existing laws did not prohibit such an act would not properly be considered a "law." What is striking about Blackstone's definition is that nowhere does he claim that a law that meets his criteria might nevertheless not be a "law" because it is unjust or substantively unreasonable, nor do the key players in the various constitutional struggles over due process and Magna Carta between 1215 and 1628 make such a claim.[36]

In short, deprivations of life, liberty, or property required express warrant in *law*, and such laws had to be *prospective* and *prescribed* rules known to the subjects. Due process of law meant first and foremost that no person could be deprived of rights without the benefit of known and established laws. Blackstone further confirmed that due process required proceedings known to the law: "Not only the substantial part, or judicial decisions, of the law, but also the formal part, or method of proceeding, cannot be altered but by parliament." Any new court "must proceed according to the old established forms of the common law," and deprivations of liberty or property "ought to be tried and determined in the ordinary courts of justice, and by course of law."[37]

DUE PROCESS OF LAW IN AMERICA

Americans inherited the English concept of due process of law. The Bill of Rights ratified in 1791 and added to the Constitution of 1789 included, in its Fifth Amendment, that "[n]o person shall ... be deprived of life, liberty, or property, without due process of law."[38] Almost all of the American states also had their own equivalent "due process" or "law of the land" clauses in their constitutions.[39] Importantly, the federal Bill of Rights (as well as the state bills of rights) also included a host of procedural protections such as trial by jury. Once enshrined in the fundamental law, these procedural protections would be required not only by the particular provisions of the constitution providing for them, but also by the due process clause.

The state and federal due process clauses were enforced and interpreted by many courts, both state and federal. These judicial opinions reveal an understanding of due process consistent with the thesis that due process required known laws and the minimum of procedure established by the Constitution or otherwise known to the law.

The Supreme Court did not decide a case under the Fifth Amendment due process clause until 1852,[40] and it did not decide a prominent case until 1856.[41] But in 1819 it heard a celebrated argument by Daniel Webster in *Trustees of Dartmouth College v. Woodward.*[42] When, by means of special legislation, the state of New Hampshire tried to revoke the rights and privileges of Dartmouth College that an old royal charter had granted to it, Webster argued that the legislature had assumed a "judicial power." It "declares a forfeiture, and resumes franchises, once granted, without trial or hearing." If the Constitution "be not altogether waste paper," Webster argued, then it must mean that the legislature cannot judge, decide, or deprive "by act," leaving "all these things to be tried and adjudged by the law of the land."[43]

Webster continued with an explanation of the "law of the land":

> By the law of the land is most clearly intended the general law; a law, which hears before it condemns; which proceeds upon inquiry, and renders judgment only after trial. The meaning is, that every citizen shall hold his life, liberty, property, and immunities, under the protection of the general rules which govern society. Every thing which may pass under the form of an enactment, is not, therefore, to be considered the law of the land. If this were so, acts of attainder, bills of pains and penalties, acts of confiscation, acts reversing judgments, and acts directly transferring one man's estate to

another, legislative judgments, decrees, and forfeitures, in all possible forms, would be the law of the land.[44]

Here, one of the most famous lawyers and statesmen of antebellum America understood due process of law to require known and established laws ("the protection of the general rules which govern society"), as well as known and established procedures (procedures of "inquiry" and "judgment only after trial"). Thomas Cooley, in his famous and well-known 1868 treatise, claimed that perhaps "[n]o definition" of due process of law "is more often quoted than that by Mr. Webster in the Dartmouth College case."[45] By this definition, legislatures could not act like courts and decide by legislative act particular controversies between individuals or deprive a subject of life, liberty, or property. Such disputes had to be resolved, and such deprivations had to occur, only according to established law.

Thomas Cooley himself was one of the most preeminent lawyers and judges of the late antebellum period, and his 1868 *Treatise on the Constitutional Limitations which Rest upon the Legislative Power of the States of the American Union* was well known and well received.[46] It was published in the same year that the Fourteenth Amendment was adopted. Cooley's treatise is useful because it was the earliest attempt at a broad-based compilation of state-level cases interpreting the state and federal constitutions. In his chapter on due process and the "law of the land," Cooley argued that one of "[t]he chief restriction[s]" of the due process clauses "is that vested rights must not be disturbed."[47] If a right has vested in a particular individual according to the existing legal rules, then a legislative act taking away that right or reassigning it would violate due process because such a deprivation would not be done according to preexisting, established laws.

This seems to be what the Supreme Court meant in its first due process case, when it interpreted a statutory extension of a patent term to apply to the patent licensee's use of the patent. "The right to construct and use" the patented invention "had been purchased and paid for without any limitation as to the time for which they were to be used," the Court explained. "They were the property of the respondents. Their only value consists in their use. And a special act of

Congress, passed afterwards, depriving the appellees of the right to use them, certainly could not be regarded as due process of law."[48]

Justice Samuel Chase's famous 1798 opinion in *Calder v. Bull*[49] seems to have understood the concept to prohibit a legislature from depriving someone of vested rights by special act, although Chase was not interpreting a due process provision and was purporting instead to articulate a matter of general principle. "A law that punished a citizen for an innocent action, or, in other words, for an act, which, when done, was in violation of no existing law . . . or a law that takes property from A and gives it to B" would not properly be called a "law." The legislature "may declare new crimes," "establish rules of conduct for all its citizens in future cases," and "command what is right, and prohibit what is wrong," but "[it] cannot change innocence into guilt; or punish innocence as a crime; or violate the right of an antecedent lawful private contract; or the right of private property."[50]

There is one passage in Cooley's important treatise that, at first glance, seems to support substantive due process, which, again, is the idea that the clause also imposes limits on the substance of legislation. "[T]he whole community," Cooley wrote, is "entitled at all times to demand the protection of the ancient principles which shield private rights against *arbitrary interference*, even though such interference may be under a rule impartial in its application."[51] This passage may seem to support the notion that courts may strike down legislation that is "arbitrary" in the sense of being substantively unreasonable.[52]

But this is not what Cooley meant by arbitrary. The case he cited for the proposition declared that the due process and law of the land clauses were "intended to secure the individual from the arbitrary exercise of the powers of government, *unrestrained by the established principles* of private rights and distributive justice."[53] Arbitrary power is rule by mere *will*, as opposed to rule by *established laws*. That was how John Locke had also defined arbitrary power in his Second Treatise. "Absolute Arbitrary Power," Locke wrote, was "Governing without *settled standing Laws*." Men would not leave the state of nature if "their Lives, Liberties and Fortunes" were not secured "by *stated Rules* of Right and Property." Thus, Locke wrote, "the Ruling Power ought to govern by *declared* and *received Laws*, and not by extemporary Dictates and undetermined Resolutions," and such power "ought not to be *Arbitrary* and at Pleasure," but rather "ought to be exercised by *established and promulgated Laws.*"[54] Or, as he put it elsewhere, "The *Legislative*, or Supream Authority, cannot assume to its self a power to Rule by extemporary Arbitrary Decrees, but is *bound to dispense Justice*, and decide the Rights of the Subject *by promulgated standing Laws, and known Authoris'd Judges.*"[55]

Due process of law, in sum, prohibits arbitrary *power* – arbitrary *acts* of the legislature that affect life, liberty, or property contrary to the existing standing laws. That is how preeminent lawyers, judges, and statesmen understood the concept from the Founding of the Republic through 1868, the year of the Fourteenth Amendment's adoption.

THE LEGISLATIVE POWER OVER PROCESS

The requirement that there be established, standing laws appears to have transferred unaltered from the English to the American constitutional system. The *process* that was required to adjudicate a deprivation, however, may have required some translation from the old to the new order. According to Blackstone, Parliament could change the proceedings necessary for certain deprivations because Parliament was the supreme legislative authority of the realm; hence he wrote that the "method of proceeding, cannot be altered *but by parliament.*"[56] Due process meant that the king could not, on his own, alter those proceedings. Put another way, Parliament, if it wished, could do away with Magna Carta entirely.[57]

Unlike the English constitutional system, the American constitutional system includes written constitutions superior and antecedent to the legislative power. Thus American courts settled on the principle that legislatures could not change what process was due once "due process of law" became a fixed constitutional requirement. Thus not only did the states have to follow whatever procedures were established in the written constitutions themselves, but also they could not abrogate the minimum procedural requirements that existed at common law for particular kinds of cases. Cooley expressed this principle when he wrote that "[a]dministrative and remedial process may change from time to time, but only with due regard to the old landmarks established for the protection of the citizen."[58]

The Supreme Court held as much in *Murray's Lessee*. The question was whether the government could use summary proceedings, authorized by Congress, to recover money allegedly embezzled from the government by a customs collector. The Court first held that the advent of written constitutions now meant that Congress could not make up whatever procedures it wished:

> It is manifest that it was not left to the legislative power to enact any process which might be devised. The article [the due process clause] is a restraint on the legislative as well as on the executive and judicial powers of the government, and cannot be so construed as to leave congress free to make any process 'due process of law,' by its mere will.[59]

The Court first held that the specific procedures in the Constitution had to be followed.[60] This would make the "process" required by due process redundant of the several constitutional provisions touching on criminal and civil process, such as the right to a jury trial and the privilege against self-incrimination.[61] But the Constitution arguably says nothing about proceedings to recover money from administrative officers the government claims have embezzled that money. The Court thus proceeded to "look to those settled usages and modes of proceeding existing in the common and statute law of England" before the adoption of the Constitution, which proceedings "are shown not to have been unsuited to [the] civil and political condition" of America.[62] The legislature could not abrogate the procedures that were used for this kind of case at common law in England, as appropriately adapted to the situation of America. The Court concluded that there was no violation because summary proceedings had existed at common law.[63]

"SUBSTANTIVE" DUE PROCESS IN ANTEBELLUM LAW

As we have seen in this chapter, due process of law was not a substantive limitation on legislatures except insofar as they could not act like courts and could not abrogate whatever procedures were determined to be fundamental for the protection of the citizen. Yet, as mentioned at the beginning of this chapter, several originalists claim that antebellum courts developed a concept of "substantive" due process – the idea that due process clauses also imposed limits on the *substance* of what legislatures could enact. There are at least three versions of this argument: States were limited to reasonable exercises of the "police powers"; states were prohibited from making class legislation, thereby suggesting an antidiscrimination component to due process; and the antislavery constitutionalists developed a theory of due process that protected fundamental rights. Briefly, none of these versions of due process is compelling.

Police Powers

The police powers were understood to be the legitimate powers of the state to regulate for the health, safety, and morals of the people. In the era of *Lochner* (the case striking down a maximum-hours law for bakers), the Court would routinely hold that states were generally limited to reasonable and legitimate exercises of their police powers.

But the antebellum doctrines did not support such a concept of substantive due process. As I have argued at length elsewhere,[64] state courts routinely invalidated *municipal* bylaws for being "unreasonable" or in excess of the police powers to regulate for the health, safety, and morals of the local citizenry. They did so because municipalities exercised only those police powers expressly delegated by the state and because, as municipal corporations, the courts subjected them to the common law of corporations. According to this common law, courts could void corporate acts if they were unreasonable, contrary to the general good of the corporation, or in restraint of trade. Neither rationale applied, nor did courts apply them, to acts of the state legislatures themselves.[65]

There were, however, at least two other doctrines that did limit state legislatures to reasonable exercises of the police powers. These doctrines existed where state power might come into potential collision with federal constitutional requirements. Thus, on the assumption that the federal commerce power was exclusive, federal courts sometimes invalidated state legislative acts affecting interstate or foreign commerce if they were not genuinely for a police powers purpose. If they were not for a legitimate police powers purpose, they were not considered regulations of police, but rather regulations of interstate commerce prohibited to the states by the (dormant) commerce clause.[66] Similarly, the Constitution prohibited states from impairing contractual obligations, but courts routinely held that states could alter ongoing contractual obligations if doing so was legitimately for a police powers purpose.[67] But these limits on state power did not apply to acts of state legislatures regulating solely internal commerce or local matters or which affected no existing contracts.

There are, however, two cases that are often believed to be exceptions in which antebellum courts appeared to adopt a substantive version of due process of law. In *Wynehamer v. People*,[68] the New York Court of Appeals invalidated a state prohibition on selling liquor as applied to liquor that existed before the statute's enactment.[69] James Ely described this case as "the first time that a court determined that the concept of due process prevented the legislature from regulating the beneficial enjoyment of property in such a manner as to destroy its value."[70] The other case is infamous for advancing a vision of substantive due process at the federal level: *Dred Scott v. Sandford*,[71] in which the Supreme Court held that Congress could not, without violating due process of law, prohibit slave owners from carrying their slave "property" into the federal territories.[72]

Several points suggest that these two cases were aberrations, however. First, they involve the rare circumstance of a total or near-total prohibition on possessing, or elimination of the value of, a species of property that had been obtained lawfully under previously existing laws. Most of the police powers cases involved something else entirely, such as regulations on butchering, selling in the market, and freedom of contract.[73] A total prohibition on a type of property previously obtained lawfully is as close to a direct legislative deprivation as one gets – and such a deprivation does violate due process under the traditional, procedural understanding.

Second, these two cases seem to have misunderstood the due process precedents on which they were based. Due process prohibited a legislature from taking property that had already vested in "A" and giving it to "B." Property rights can be arranged only prospectively and by general, standing laws.[74] *Wynehamer* and *Dred Scott* were the first cases to hold that, at least as applied to existing property that had already been obtained lawfully, there were some *types* of property that could simply not be prohibited by legislation. Indeed, Thomas Cooley, in his treatise, explained that many liquor prohibitions had been sustained by state courts. As a result of such legislation, "the merchant of yesterday becomes the criminal of to-day, and the very building in which he lives and conducts the business which to that moment was lawful becomes perhaps a nuisance, if the statute shall so declare, and liable to be proceeded against for a forfeiture."[75] Legislatures *were* allowed to prohibit certain species of property; the *Wynehamer* and *Dred Scott* courts simply got the doctrine wrong.

Third, these two cases were widely condemned at the time. John Hart Ely argued that "*Wynehamer* and the *Dred Scott* reference were aberrations, neither precedented nor destined to become precedents themselves," and that "[o]ther courts on which they were urged were quite acid in the judgment that they had misused the constitutional language by giving it a substantive reading."[76] In short, the police powers cases and the two famous cases in which complete prohibitions on specific types of property were invalidated simply do not support the thesis that antebellum courts enforced a substantive version of due process of law.

Class Legislation

A variant of the substantive due process argument is that due process prohibited class legislation – that is, legislation that favored one class of people over another.[77] The argument for this understanding of due process is also weak. Almost all of the cases purporting to support it come from a single state, Tennessee.[78] Only two of the cases from Tennessee, however, actually appear to hold that due process prohibits "partial" legislation that affects only a small number of individuals, as opposed to a "general" law applicable to all.[79] The others can all be understood under traditional understandings of due process. For example, although there is some language in the 1831 case *Wally's Heirs v. Kennedy*[80] suggesting that partial laws are invalid, at issue in that case was an act of the legislature purporting to eliminate claims that were being pursued in preexisting, already-filed court cases, suggesting the legislature was trying to direct the outcomes in specific cases.[81] In the same year, *Bank of the State v. Cooper*[82] involved the creation of a unique judicial process for a particular class of bank debtors with no right of appeal.[83] And in 1836 *Jones' Heirs v. Perry*[84] involved an act of the state legislature directing an estate to sell lands to pay off the decedent's creditors – or, as the court put it, the legislature "adjudge[d] the existence of the debts, and decree[d] that the lands be sold for their payment."[85] This was nothing but a "judicial decree" masquerading as a "law."[86]

The leading 1829 case on which these other cases relied, *Vanzant v. Waddel*,[87] involved a state law creating a unique process for recovering debts owed to certain banks – and the state law was, of all things, upheld. The court distinguished the legislative act in that case from the one in *Darmouth College* by noting that, in the latter case, the legislature had tried to resolve a judicial case in favor of one of the particular parties – a violation of due process on the traditional understanding. Additionally, two judges writing separately explained what they understood to be "partial" laws: "The idea of a people through their representatives making laws whereby are swept away the life, liberty and property of *one* or a *few* citizens," they wrote, "is too odious to be tolerated in any government where freedom has a name."[88] These partial laws, in other words, were laws that directly deprived select individuals of life, liberty, or property – exactly what is prohibited by the traditional procedural understanding of due process.

Scholars have also relied on statements from a few other state courts to the effect that due process prohibited special or partial laws, but none supports the proposition; each can also be explained on a traditional understanding of due process of law. For example, in *Reed v. Wright*,[89] a case from Iowa in 1849, the court wrote that "[l]aws affecting life, liberty and property must be general in their application, operating upon the entire community alike."[90] That case involved an act, however, that directly eliminated judicial process for a select group of individuals who already owned particular tracts of lands; it was a "special and limited act confined to a particular class of individuals, by which they were to be deprived of their property."[91] These individuals could be divested of their lands, the court held, only "by judicial proceedings according to the course of the common law."[92] And in *Janes v. Reynolds' Adm'rs*,[93] an 1847 case out of Texas in which the court mentioned that the "laws of the land" were "general" as opposed to "partial" laws,[94] the court dealt with a statute that directly eliminated notice and jury trial rights for particular kinds of claims. This statute implicated not class legislation, but the traditional understanding of due process – and the court upheld the statute at that.[95]

In short, many of these so-called class legislation cases are consistent with traditional, procedural due process. They involved legislative abrogation of judicial process or a legislature decreeing specific outcomes in judicial cases. The scholars who cite these cases as support for the proposition that due process prohibited class legislation appear to be confused by the fact that, in most of them, the legislature worked a direct deprivation of property or abrogated judicial procedures for a specific class of individuals only. For that reason, these laws were often "partial," but they were ultimately classic due process cases and not matters of class legislation as such.

Antislavery Constitutionalism

Finally, some scholars have argued that cases such as *Wynehamer* and *Dred Scott* reflected a changed public understanding of due process as a result of antislavery ideology. This began when the *proponents* of slavery argued that depriving masters of their slave property by law would be to deprive them of property without due process of law.[96] They made this argument in support of their agenda to deny Congress any power to prohibit slavery in the territories or the District of Columbia, notwithstanding Congress's clear power to make all "needful" regulations for the territories and to exercise "exclusive" legislation over the District.[97]

The antislavery advocates struck back. If anything, slavery itself violates due process because it deprives people of liberty and their property in their own labor with no process at all. Randy Barnett has catalogued many antislavery constitutionalists making such arguments.[98] For example, Theodore Dwight Weld argued in 1838 that "[a]ll the slaves in the District have been 'deprived of liberty' by legislative acts. Now these legislative acts 'depriving' them 'of liberty' were either 'due process of law' or they were *not*." It is "granted" that due process is judicial process, and "no slave in the District has been deprived of his liberty by 'a judicial process,' or, in other words, by 'due process of law.' "[99] Alvan Stewart wrote in 1837 that "the true and only meaning of the phrase, 'due process of law,' is an indictment or presentment by a grand jury, of not less than twelve men, and a judgment pronounced on the finding of the jury, by a court," adding that, of course, "there is not a slave at this moment, in the United States" who has become a slave according to these procedures.[100]

William Goodell similarly argued that any person "deprived of liberty without indictment, jury trial, and judgment of Court, is therefore UNCONSTITUTIONALLY deprived of liberty."[101] In the context of the fugitive slave laws, Salmon P. Chase argued, "Now, unless it can be shewn that no process of law at all, is the same thing as due process of law, it must be admitted that the act which authorizes seizure without process, is repugnant to a constitution which expressly forbids it."[102] The Republican Party Platform of 1860 summed this all up: because the Founding Fathers "ordained that 'no persons should be deprived of life, liberty or property without due process of law,' . . . we deny the authority of Congress, of a territorial legislature, or of any individuals, to give legal existence to slavery in any territory of the United States."[103]

These abolitionist arguments about the meaning of due process do not seem to support substantive due process at all. Although the Republican Party platform is admittedly a bit vague, every single statement from the famous abolitionists relies entirely on the procedural understanding of due process. Indeed, people were made slaves by no order of any court. More still, they violated no preexisting law. They were made slaves simply because the law directed that the mere *existence* of these individuals was sufficient to render them subject to the forced violence of slavery. But the requirement of established law means that people must have it within their power not to violate that law at all and thus to avoid the punishment. Otherwise, the requirement of established law is a mockery. If it is literally impossible to avoid violating a law, then it would be no different than the legislature directly depriving someone of liberty and property. Put another way, a law that punishes for an immutable characteristic is not "law" within the procedural meaning of due process of law. And a law authorizing the enslavement of individuals on the basis of characteristics outside their control is not such a "law" either.[104]

To be sure, if the abolitionists were correct, then Congress never had the power to permit slavery in the territories. It would mean that the Founders, who in 1787 assumed that Congress would have power to control slavery in the territories as it saw fit, unwittingly prohibited slavery everywhere except in the individual states where it already existed by adding the Fifth Amendment in 1791. Of course, it could be that Congress did not fully understand the implications of adding a due process clause to the Constitution.[105] But even if the abolitionists were wrong that slavery in fact violated due process of law, they would have been wrong merely on the lower-order results. Their definitions of due process of law are best read as entirely conventional. At least, nothing in their statements compels a substantive reading of due process of law.

CONCLUSION

In conclusion, "due process of law" at the time of the ratification of the Fourteenth Amendment had a specific historical and legal meaning. The best reading of the evidence is that this meaning was that no individual could be deprived of life, liberty, or property without first having violated existing, established law and without the benefit of the critical procedures historically used for determining the violation of such laws, including the several procedures specifically mentioned by the federal Constitution. Very little in the antebellum sources supports a substantive component to due process of law.

2 PROTECTION OF THE LAWS

"The very essence of civil liberty certainly consists in the right of every individual to claim the protection of the laws, whenever he receives an injury. One of the first duties of government is to afford that protection."

John Marshall, Marbury v. Madison (1803)

The equal protection clause of the Fourteenth Amendment, like the due process clause, is often treated today as a broad and open-ended provision that requires courts to import their own values and sense of equality over time. Most constitutional litigation related to the Fourteenth Amendment involves one of these two clauses. But, as with the due process clause, the equal protection clause is not quite as broad and open-ended as the Supreme Court seems to say. It turns out that the legal concept "protection of the laws" also has deep historical and even philosophical roots. There is no doubt that the equal protection clause requires equality – but with respect to what? Does it mean that all laws must be "equal"? That all laws affording privileges and benefits must do so equally?

This chapter shows that the provision does require equality in something very important, but the required equality is narrower than modern interpretations would suggest. The clause requires equality in the *protection of the laws*. This was a legal concept intimately related to due process of law. Due process of law provides the rules for how the *government* can deprive a subject or citizen of natural rights to life, liberty, and property. The protection of the laws is the concept that requires government to protect these same rights from *private interference*. It is the protection the government accords its subjects and citizens, primarily through physical protection and judicial remedies, so they may exercise and enjoy their rights without the interference of others.

THE POLITICAL THEORY OF THE FOUNDING

It may seem odd to start this discussion with the political theory of the Founding generation. Yet the concept of the protection of the laws is intimately connected with that political theory – particularly the transition from the political theory of the ancient philosophers to the early modern thinkers such as Thomas Hobbes, John Locke, and William Blackstone.

As twentieth-century political thinker Martin Diamond explained, the various political theorists of the ancient world maintained that the object of any given regime was the cultivation of virtue. For example, many "political theories had ranked highly, as objects of government, the nurturing of a particular religion, education, military courage, civic-spiritedness, moderation, individual excellence in the virtues, etc."[1] Aristotle and the ancient philosophers understood the *polis* – the city or city-state – "as an association for the formation of character."[2] This objective "helps us to understand something of the harsh demands of the classical teaching" – that is, "the general sternness of the laws; the emphasis placed on rigorous and comprehensive programs of education; the strict regulation of much that we now deem 'private'; the necessity of civic piety; ... and the severe restrictions on private economic activity."[3]

That the aim of the city (the political community) was a kind of virtue can be seen most clearly from Aristotle's description of the origins and ends of the city in Book 3 of *The Politics*: "[M]an is by nature a political animal. Hence [men] strive to live together even when they have no need of assistance from one another, though it is also the case that the common advantage brings them together, to the extent that it falls to each to live finely."[4] People do not form society for the protection of their rights – they form society even when they have no need of assistance from one another – but they come together rather for the purpose of living a full and complete human existence. According to Aristotle, if individuals entered into society merely "to prevent their suffering injustice from anyone" or "for purposes of exchange and of use of one another," then a polity would be no different than an alliance of remote allies.[5]

"It is evident, therefore," writes Aristotle, "that the city is not a partnership in a location and for the sake of not committing injustice against each other and of transacting business," but "for the sake of a complete and self-sufficient life."[6] Aristotle concludes that "[l]iving well, then, is the end of the city," that "[a] city is the partnership of families and villages in a complete and self-sufficient life," and that a complete and self-sufficient life is "living happily and finely." Thus the city exists "for the sake of noble actions," not merely "for the sake of living together."[7]

The early modern philosophers took a different approach. They deemphasized, without completing rejecting, the higher aims of political life and civil society; society was, first and foremost, created not for the sake of living *well* (i.e., nobly and virtuously), but rather for the sake of protecting natural rights. Beginning with Thomas Hobbes, these early modern thinkers argued that the end of civil society was the remedying of the defects and inconveniences of the state of nature. The state of nature that existed before any civil society was a state of perpetual war "of every man, against every man," wrote Hobbes.[8] Individuals agreed to restrain themselves through the creation of a commonwealth, or state, because of their "foresight of their own preservation, and of a more contented life thereby; that is to say, of getting themselves out from that miserable condition of Warre."[9] The "end" of such a commonwealth is for men "to live peaceably amongst themselves, *and be protected against other men.*"[10]

John Locke, who was tremendously influential on the Founders, similarly argued that the "great and *chief end*" of individuals uniting into commonwealths "and putting themselves under Government, *is the Preservation of their Property,*" which Locke defined as their "Lives, Liberties and Estates."[11] The "intention" of one's entering into civil society is "the better to preserve himself his Liberty and Property," for "no rational Creature can be supposed to change his condition with an intention to be worse."[12] Hence the "power of the Society, or *Legislative* constituted by them, . . . is obliged to secure every one[']s Property by providing against" the defects of the state of nature, where life, liberty, and property are not secure due to the want of known laws, indifferent judges, and an executive power to enforce the rules.[13]

The Declaration of Independence is, of course, a decidedly Lockean document:

> We hold these truths to be self-evident, that all men are created equal, that they are endowed by their Creator with certain unalienable Rights, that among these are Life, Liberty and the pursuit of Happiness. – That to secure these rights, Governments are instituted among Men, deriving their just powers from the consent of the governed, – That whenever any Form of Government becomes destructive of these ends, it is the Right of the People to alter or to abolish it, and to institute new Government, laying its foundation on such principles and organizing its powers in such form, as to them shall seem most likely to effect their Safety and Happiness.

The very aim of civil society is the preservation of life, liberty, and the ability to acquire and possess property for survival, comfort, and happiness. The *Federalist Papers*, too, explain that the "first object of government" is the "*protection* of" the "diversity in the faculties of men, from which the rights of property originate."[14] Note, however, that this primary object does not preclude the virtue sought by the ancients; the signers of the Declaration of Independence certainly believed that the protection for natural rights was a precondition for "happiness," which was the ultimate end sought by many of the ancient political philosophers.

Still, the emphasis of the modern thinkers is not on virtue, but rather on protection for rights. Martin Diamond summarizes this transition from ancient to modern political philosophy: "Blaming classical and medieval thought for adhering to dangerous illusions regarding the way men *ought* to live, that is, for trying to shape human character by misleading and unachievable standards of perfection," Diamond explains, "the new, or modern political philosophers purported to base their views and recommendations upon the character of man 'as he actually *is*.' "[15] The modern philosophers substituted the utopian end of politics with "a lowered political end, namely, human comfort and security."[16] "Not to instruct and to transcend [men's] passions and interests, but rather to channel and to use them became the hallmark of modern politics."[17] The very idea of "government" as opposed to a "polity," writes Diamond, was "a response to this restriction in the scope of the political."[18] The American government, Diamond contends, was rooted in this "solid but low foundation" – the protection of rights and the channeling of self-interest and passion – as opposed to the "premodern perspective" that unrealistically aimed at the inculcation of virtue through politics.[19]

We can now start to see what the concept "protection of the laws" might have entailed. It was the protection that government afforded to an individual's natural rights to life, liberty, and property; it was the protection that individuals sought for their natural rights by entering into civil society. Blackstone's *Commentaries*, which we encountered in Chapter 1, makes this unequivocal. In the same chapter on the absolute rights of individuals, Blackstone explained that "the principal aim of society is to *protect* individuals in the enjoyment of those absolute rights, ... which could not be preserved in peace without that mutual assistance and intercourse, which is gained by the institution of friendly and social communities." It follows "that the first and primary end of human laws is to maintain and regulate these *absolute* rights of individuals."[20] Therefore, wrote Blackstone, "the principal view of human laws is, or ought always to be, to explain, *protect*, and enforce such rights."[21] In the state of nature, in contrast, where every man retains "the absolute and uncontroled power of doing whatever he pleases, ... there would be no security to individuals in any of the enjoyments of life."[22]

Indeed, the "spirit of liberty is so deeply implanted in our [the British] constitution," wrote Blackstone, that the moment a slave lands in England, he "falls under the *protection of the laws*, and with regard to all natural rights becomes *eo instanti* a freeman."[23] What, here, is the "protection of the laws"? It is the protection the law extends to the former slave's *natural rights*: the rights to life, liberty, and to acquire, possess, and enjoy property. No subject can take away these rights by enslaving another nor can any subject take another's life away without express warrant in law. Life "cannot legally be disposed of or destroyed by any individual, neither by the person himself nor by any other of his fellow creatures, merely upon their own authority."[24] Life could only be "forfeited for the breach of those laws of society, which are enforced by the sanction of capital punishments," and only according to due process of law. "[T]he constitution is an utter stranger to any arbitrary power of killing or maiming the subject without the express warrant of law," wrote Blackstone, and "no man shall be forejudged of life or limb, contrary to the great charter and the law of the land," or "be put to death, without being brought to answer by due process of law."[25]

Here, then, we see the intimate connection between due process of law and the protection of the laws. Both are necessary in a civil society entered into for the purpose of securing natural rights. The protection of the laws is the protection the law accords to natural rights against private interference – the protection against the depredations of one's fellow man. It remedies the defects of the state of nature, where the natural rights to life, liberty, and property are insecure. Due process of law then provides the only legitimate vehicle by which such rights might be forfeited: only by the state, and only according to known laws and known procedures.

We see this connection, too, when Blackstone speaks of imprisonment: "The confinement of the person, in any wise, is an imprisonment. So that the keeping a man against his will in a private house, putting him in the stocks, arresting or forcibly detaining him in the street, is an imprisonment."[26] Blackstone continued:

> To make imprisonment lawful, it must either be, by process from the courts of judicature, or by warrant from some legal officer, having authority to commit to prison; which warrant must be in writing, under the hand and seal of the magistrate, and express the causes of the commitment, in order to be examined into (if necessary) upon a *habeas corpus.*[27]

No private individual can imprison another; the law protects individuals against private interference with one's enjoyment of liberty as well as life. Only the government can make an imprisonment lawful and only by the known processes of the law.

Blackstone concluded with the observation that the (British) constitution has "established certain other auxiliary subordinate rights of the subject, which serve principally as barriers to protect and maintain inviolate the three great and primary rights, of personal security, personal liberty, and private property."[28] Among these is the right of "applying to the courts of justice for redress of injuries"; because the law is "the supreme arbiter of every man's life, liberty, and property, courts of justice must at all times be open to the subject, and the law be duly administered therein."[29] Indeed, Magna Carta guarantees not only due process of law, but also that "[t]o no one will we sell, to no one deny or delay right or justice."[30] Here, Blackstone quotes Sir Edward Coke, who explained that, by this provision of the Great Charter, "every subject, ... for injury done to him *in bonis, in terris, vel persona,* by any other subject, ... may take his remedy by the course of the law, and have justice and right for the injury done to him, freely without sale, fully without any denial, and speedily without delay."[31]

The central idea of this concept is, as Coke explained, that individuals would have a *remedy* for injuries done to them by others. Protection of the laws, in other words, was centrally about the remedial function of the law. An earlier passage from Blackstone puts the question beyond all doubt:

> The *remedial* part of a law is so necessary a consequence of the [declaratory and directory parts of the law], that laws must be very vague and imperfect without it. For in vain would rights be declared, in vain directed to be observed, if there were no method of recovering and asserting those rights, when wrongfully withheld or invaded. This is what we mean properly, when we speak of the protection of the law.[32]

In short, due process of law and the protection of the laws are intimately connected concepts.[33] Both are necessary in a society dedicated to the preservation and securing of natural rights. The protection of the laws is the protection in the enjoyment of such rights that the law accords against private interference; due process of law is the corollary concept that establishes the only legitimate way in which a subject *may* be deprived of such rights. The key point is that the requirements of due process and the protection of the laws do not *define* the scope or content of any liberty or property interest. They stand for the proposition that whatever liberty and property interests exist according to law, the government must ensure that we may enjoy those rights and interests free of private interference and free of arbitrary deprivation by the government.

PROTECTION OF THE LAWS IN AMERICA

This seems to have been the understanding of "protection of the laws," as well as "equal protection," in American legal documents and cases. To take but one prominent example, Chief Justice John Marshall wrote in *Marbury v. Madison*, "The very essence of civil liberty certainly consists in the right of every individual to claim the protection of the laws, whenever he receives an injury. One of the first duties of government is to afford that protection."[34]

Philip Hamburger observes that there are numerous references to "equal protection" in early documents relating to religious sects.[35] One of the earliest reference is the Massachusetts Constitution of 1780, which provided that "every denomination of Christians, demeaning themselves peaceably and as good subjects of the commonwealth, shall be equally under the protection of the law."[36] Although not defining the term in that clause, elsewhere that constitution's due process clause provided, among other guarantees, that "[n]o subject shall be . . . put out of the protection of the law . . . but by the judgment of his peers, or the law of the land."[37] Blackstone defined this exact phrase, "put out of the protection of the law," as the condition of "outlawry," meaning that the outlaw "is incapable of taking the benefit of [the law] in any respect, either by bringing actions or otherwise."[38] The Massachusetts Constitution of 1780 therefore used the concept "equally under the protection of the law" in the same manner in which Blackstone had used it: as a reference to remedies in court for violations done by others.

In an important paper, Christopher Green comprehensively demonstrates that, between the early 1600s and 1866 (the year in which the Fourteenth Amendment was drafted), the phrase "protection of the laws" was used to refer to the remedial and protective services of government.[39] This is consistent with the view described above and suggests that the "equal protection of the laws" does not refer to equal laws in the sense that all laws must confer benefits equally.

Most interesting for our purposes is Green's observation that, historically, the protection of the laws was understood to apply to all persons and not only to citizens. This is important because the

Fourteenth Amendment prohibits a state from abridging the privileges or immunities of "citizens," but the due process clause protects all *persons*, and the equal protection clause protects all persons "within" a state's "jurisdiction." This would make a lot of sense. Citizenship may entail a whole set of privileges that do not apply to foreigners or aliens, but the protection of the laws must apply to all persons, for all persons have natural rights that all governments are bound to respect. Hence, Green explains, so long as a foreigner or alien in the country obeyed the laws of the realm, he came within the "protection" of the sovereign.[40]

This theory of reciprocity between allegiance and protection follows exactly from the premises of the natural rights thinkers. Individuals exit the state of nature and enter civil society *by* giving up their natural freedom to be laws unto themselves and judges in their own causes; in exchange for this obedience to the general rules of the new community, that community remedies the defects of the state of nature by according the protection to natural rights that was previously wanting.

There are even a few instances of the phrase "equal protection" – and "equal protection of the laws" – from the first quarter of the nineteenth century that predate the Fourteenth Amendment. Most usages, even in court cases, seem purely incidental or accidental. But some are quite relevant, and they refer to "equal protection" as equality in the remedial function of the laws. In *Henry v. Thompson* (1824),[41] for example, one advocate argued to the Alabama Supreme Court that "[i]f the harmony of society and the rights and happiness of its members, are to be protected by those who administer the laws intended for the equal protection of all, judicial remedies must of necessity keep pace with fraudulent ingenuity." And in *Baker v. Lovett* (1809),[42] the Supreme Judicial Court of Massachusetts held that "all infants are entitled to equal protection" for "an injury done."

The term also appears in John Adams' seventh *Novanglus* essay from 1774 and the 1800 trial of John Fries for treason, for his involvement in the eponymous Fries Rebellion in Pennsylvania. In both instances, the term is used in connection with the "allegiance for protection" theory. In *Novanglus*, Adams explains the meaning of the writers on the laws of nations on the status of the colonial possessions:

"[T]he new country shall have equal right, powers, and privileges, as well as equal protection, and be under equal obligations of obedience, with the old."[43] Here, importantly, equal protection is distinct from equal rights and privileges.

As for the Fries trial, Supreme Court Justice Samuel Chase, presiding over the trial as a district court judge, delivered the following speech to John Fries and his fellow defendants after the jury convicted them, explaining to them the nature of their crime and why they had no right to rebel against the general government:

> You are a native of this country – you live under a constitution (or form of government) framed by the people themselves; and under laws made by your representatives, faithfully executed by independent and impartial judges. Your government secures to every member of the community equal liberty and equal rights; by which equality of liberty and rights, I mean, that every person, without any regard to wealth, rank, or station, may enjoy an equal share of civil liberty, and equal protection of law, and an equal security for his person and property.[44]

Justice Chase immediately went on to say that if Fries and his cohort had believed the Constitution against which they had rebelled to be defective, "[t]he people themselves have established the mode by which such grievances are to be redressed; and no other mode can be adopted without a violation of the constitution and of the laws."[45]

Can there be any clearer statement of the "allegiance for protection" theory derived from the early modern thinkers about the state of nature and origins of civil society? The people themselves have formed a society and have given up a portion of their natural freedom to better secure their natural rights; so long as the government offers "equal protection of law" – so long as the government grants the protection of the laws for one's life, liberty, and property equally to all – no person has a right to rebel against that government.

Finally, this is also likely how Andrew Jackson used the phrase in his famous bank veto message in 1832. Some scholars rely on Jackson's veto for the proposition that "equal protection" meant something distinct from the "protection of the laws." These scholars argue that equal protection did in fact mean equal benefits and equal laws generally.[46]

Jackson attacked the Bank of the United States for being "an exclusive privilege of banking under the authority of the General Government" and "a monopoly."[47] "It is to be regretted," Jackson continued, "that the rich and powerful too often bend the acts of government to their selfish purposes." Of course, that does not mean that natural inequalities do not exist: "Distinctions in society will always exist under every just government. Equality of talents, of education, or of wealth can not be produced by human institutions. In the full enjoyment of the gifts of Heaven and the fruits of superior industry, economy, and virtue, every man," Jackson wrote, "is *equally entitled to protection by law.*" But, he added:

> ... when the laws undertake to add to these natural and just advantages artificial distinctions, to grant titles, gratuities, and exclusive privileges, to make the rich richer and the potent more powerful, the humble members of society – the farmers, mechanics, and laborers – who have neither the time nor the means of securing like favors to themselves, have a right to complain of the injustice of their Government. There are no necessary evils in government. Its evils exist only in its abuses. If it would confine itself to *equal protection,* and, as Heaven does its rains, shower its favors alike on the high and the low, the rich and the poor, it would be an unqualified blessing. In the act before me there seems to be a wide and unnecessary departure from these just principles.[48]

In this passage, "equal protection" could plausibly refer either to the equal "protection of the laws" or to "shower[ing]" government favors "alike on the high and the low." The "protection of the laws" reading seems to be the superior one. Jackson is attacking the special privileges conferred by some laws. These laws should be stricken, he says, and the government should "confine itself to equal protection." This cannot be divorced from the preceding part of the paragraph where he writes that, in the "full enjoyment of the gifts of Heaven" (i.e., in the enjoyment of natural rights), every person is "equally entitled to protection by law." Jackson here means nothing more nor less than that government should get out of the business of bestowing special privileges altogether; it should confine itself to protection for everyone's natural rights and talents.

To be sure, if government *does* confer privileges, it should do so on all alike. But that hardly equates equal protection of the laws with equal privileges generally. Indeed, when Jackson spoke later of such equal privileges in his farewell address, he used different terminology. He spoke of "men who love liberty and desire nothing but equal rights and equal laws."[49] There seems a world of difference between equal "rights" and equal "laws" and equal *protection of the laws*. Jackson's use of the latter phrase in his veto message is consistent with our prior analysis of this legal concept's meaning. Although it is surely possible to read Jackson's veto message as equating equal protection with equal privileges, at a minimum nothing compels such a reading. Simply put, the better reading, in light of all of the evidence, is that the equal protection of the laws required only that the government provide legal protection against private interference for our exercise and enjoyment of our existing rights to life, liberty, and property as defined by law.

3 THE PRIVILEGES AND IMMUNITIES OF CITIZENSHIP

"The Citizens of each State shall be entitled to all Privileges and Immunities of Citizens in the several States."

U.S. Const., art. IV, § 2, cl. 2.

The Fourteenth Amendment has three injunctions in its first section. It provides that no state shall deprive any person of life, liberty, or property without due process of law, nor deny to any person within its jurisdiction the equal protection of the laws. These two guarantees are perhaps the most litigated constitutional provisions today. And, as we have seen in the previous two chapters, due process of law and the protection of the laws were well-defined legal concepts in antebellum America, dating from well before the Founding.

The Fourteenth Amendment's first section's other injunction is less familiar to modern readers because it is almost never litigated. The Supreme Court effectively neutered the provision when the Court first interpreted it in 1873 (see Chapter 7). That injunction declares first that "[a]ll persons born or naturalized in the United States, and subject to the jurisdiction thereof, are citizens of the United States and of the State wherein they reside." It then provides that "[n]o State shall make or enforce any law which shall abridge the privileges or immunities of citizens of the United States."

This provision of the Fourteenth Amendment is undoubtedly the hardest to interpret. There are at least four plausible interpretations of this clause. Does it guarantee only the privileges and immunities of *national* citizenship, such as the guarantees of the Bill of Rights, and thus incorporate the Bill of Rights against the states? Does it guarantee all fundamental privileges and immunities, including traditionally state-defined privileges such as the right to contract and acquire property? Does it merely require *equality* in whatever privileges and immunities a state happens to accord its citizens? Or does it merely reiterate the requirement of the privileges *and* immunities clause of the original Constitution and prohibit a state from discriminating against the free citizens of other states?

Each of these views has prominent advocates in the academic literature. We shall explore these possibilities in more depth in Chapters 5 and 6. In this chapter, we shall equip ourselves to confront these possibilities by exploring the meaning of "privileges and immunities" clauses in antebellum law. As we shall see, the traditional meaning of these clauses is actually quite straightforward: they required *equality* in whatever privileges and immunities a sovereign happened to grant its citizens or to foreigners. Whether this traditional equality or comity-based understanding of the historical privileges and immunities provisions underwent a transformation in the Fourteenth Amendment is a difficult question that we address in later chapters.

FROM INTERNATIONAL TREATIES TO THE FEDERAL CONSTITUTION

Privileges and immunities clauses were first significantly elaborated in international treaties between Great Britain and other nations. These treaties usually provided that visitors to and from Britain and the country with which it was signing a treaty would enjoy a "most favored nation" status: these visitors would receive at least as many privileges and immunities as other foreign visitors received. Here is one prominent example from the seventeenth century, from a treaty between Great Britain and Portugal:

> [T]he English merchants and other subjects of the King of Great Britain shall enjoy the same, and as great privileges and immunities, as to their being imprisoned, arrested, or any other way molested in their persons, houses, books of accounts, merchandizes and goods, within the extent of the states of the most renowned King of

Portugal, as have been, or shall be for the future granted to any Prince or people in alliance with the King of Portugal.[1]

Although, here, British subjects would not necessarily benefit from the same privileges and immunities as Portuguese subjects in Portugal, they would get at least as many privileges and immunities as any other foreign peoples received upon visiting Portugal. It was, in short, an equality requirement with respect to certain privileges and immunities. In the case of this treaty, the privileges and immunities were enumerated, and they included important liberty rights such as the rights to be free from arbitrary imprisonment and arrest and from unreasonable searches and seizures.

One treaty between Britain and Sicily from the early eighteenth century noted that the Queen of Great Britain was "watchful to preserve the rights and privileges of her subjects trading in the said kingdom, and being likewise willing to preserve to the Sicilians the privileges they have in Great Britain," and so it was declared that:

> ... British merchants are henceforward to have, and shall effectually have, use, and enjoy all those rights, privileges, liberties, and entire security, as to their persons, goods, ships, seamen, trade, and navigation, in the said kingdom of Sicily, which, by virtue of the treaties made between Great Britain and Spain, they have hitherto enjoyed, or ought to enjoy; ... and if hitherto any more favourable privileges have been granted to the merchants of any other foreign nation, or shall hereafter be granted, ... the British merchants shall likewise in all respects, and in the fullest manner, enjoy the same.[2]

Other nations reportedly also used such provisions. For example, a treaty between France and Spain from 1761 reportedly provided that "their natural born subjects are to enjoy all rights, privileges and immunities, &c. in both kingdoms."[3]

Other privileges and immunities provisions in other kinds of documents were similarly about nondiscrimination. The Laws in Wales Act of 1535–36, which incorporated Wales fully into the kingdom of England, provided that (with the English modernized) "all and singular person and persons born and to be born in the said principality, country, or dominion of Wales, shall have, enjoy, and inherit all and singular freedoms, liberties, rights, privileges, and laws within this realm and other[s] [of] the king's dominions as other[s] [of] the king's subjects naturally born within the same have, enjoy, and inherit."[4]

In a similar vein, in 1608 *Calvin's Case*[5] addressed whether a subject born in Scotland after the ascension of James I in England (who had been James VI of Scotland) was entitled to the privileges and immunities of English law and citizenship or was to be treated as an alien. The defendants, who had seized some of Calvin's English lands, argued that Calvin was not entitled to the "benefits and privileges of the laws of England." Sir Edward Coke drew an analogy to Paul of Tarsus, who was born in Asia Minor, "and yet being born under the obedience of the Roman Emperor, he was by birth a citizen of Rome in Italy in Europe, that is, capable of and inheritable to all privileges and immunities of that city." The argument made against Calvin, Coke wrote, "might have made St. Paul an alien to Rome."[6]

American colonists, too, insisted that they were entitled to the same "privileges and immunities" as natural-born English citizens. Thus a 1639 Maryland law provided that the inhabitants of the province "[s]hall have and enjoy all such rights liberties immunities priviledges and free customs within this Province as any natural born subject of England hath or ought to have or enjoy in the Realm of England."[7] In the revolutionary period, the American colonies reminded the British that they were entitled to the same "privileges and immunities" as the people of Britain.[8]

To be sure, the phrase "privileges and immunities" could appear in other contexts. Many corporate charters granted a variety of "privileges" and "immunities," and these did not have to do with nondiscrimination.[9] And some treaties even simply declared what the privileges and immunities of traders would be. Thus a treaty between Great Britain and Spain in 1667 provided that "all the English merchants" trading in particular provinces "should enjoy, from henceforward, all the privileges, exemptions, immunities, and benefits, which formerly have been agreed and given" by ancient treaties between Britain and these regions.[10] Even here, it might be noted, this provision was a kind of equality or nondiscrimination requirement between two time periods.

Whatever other privileges and immunities provisions might have been out there, the treaties and acts providing for nondiscrimination

across peoples or geographies are the most relevant to the American
context after independence. How were the citizens of the various states
to be treated in the other states of the American confederation? The
Articles of Confederation provided in its fourth article that, to better
"secure and perpetuate mutual friendship and intercourse among the
people of the different States in this Union, the free inhabitants of each
of these States, paupers, vagabonds and fugitives from justice
excepted, shall be entitled to all privileges and immunities of free
citizens in the several States." It then illustrated what some of these
privileges and immunities were:

> [T]he people of each State shall have free ingress and regress to and
> from any other State, and shall enjoy therein all the privileges of
> trade and commerce, subject to the same duties, impositions and
> restrictions as the inhabitants thereof respectively, provided that
> such restrictions shall not extend so far as to prevent the removal of
> property imported into any State, to any other State of which the
> owner is an inhabitant; provided also that no imposition, duties or
> restriction shall be laid by any State, on the property of the United
> States, or either of them.[11]

This clause in the Articles, in other words, ensured interstate nondiscrimination with respect to whatever privileges and immunities a state
happened to grant its own inhabitants. The federal Constitution adopted
this provision, but also simplified it: "The Citizens of each State shall be
entitled to all Privileges and Immunities of Citizens in the several
States."[12] This clause changed "inhabitants" to "citizens," and it no
longer enumerated the various privileges and immunities presumably
because an enumeration would be both superfluous and nonexhaustive.
But its thrust was the same: this clause ensured that a citizen of a fellow
state would receive the same privileges and immunities that the state in
which he was traveling granted its own citizens. Hence this clause of the
Constitution is often called the comity clause.

On the eve of the Civil War, the New York Court of Appeals – the
state's highest court – clearly captured what the meaning of this clause
had been throughout the antebellum period. The question in *Lemmon
v. People*[13] was whether the slaves of a Virginian family traveling to
Texas via New York became free immediately upon setting foot in

New York state. A New York state law provided that any slave became instantly free upon arriving in New York; the central issue was whether this law violated the comity clause. The reader may justly express disbelief that such a question was ever really in dispute. After all, did the comity clause not require a state to provide the same privileges to out-of-state citizens that it provided to its *own* citizens? No citizen of New York was allowed to own slaves.[14]

The New York court thus easily upheld the slaves' freedom. "I think this is the first occasion in the juridical history of the country," Justice Wright observed, "that an attempt has been made to torture this provision into a guaranty of the right of a slave owner to bring his slaves into . . . a non-slaveholding State."[15] Rather, the provision:

> . . . was always understood as having but one design and meaning, viz., to secure to the citizens of every State, within every other, the privileges and immunities (whatever they might be) accorded in each to its own citizens. It was intended to guard against a State discriminating in favor of its own citizens. A citizen of Virginia coming into New York was to be entitled to all the privileges and immunities accorded to the citizens of New York. He was not to be received or treated as an alien or enemy in the particular sovereignty.[16]

Or, as another judge put it, "the meaning is, that in a given State, every citizen of every other State shall have the same privileges and immunities – that is, the same rights – which the citizens of that State possess."[17]

To be sure, the arguments in *Lemmon* suggest that the idea that the comity clause was not about discrimination, but rather protected certain absolute, fundamental rights, had some adherents in the lead-up to the Civil War.[18] In particular, Southerners relied on the clause to argue that they had the absolute right to transit through other states with their slaves.[19] Yet these arguments were widely rejected outside the South[20] and were clearly products of motivated reasoning. Indeed, those advocating for the absolute rights of slave owners implausibly denied at the same time any absolute right on the part of abolitionists to speak freely or of free blacks to enjoy the basic rights of citizenship in the South.[21]

It is also true that some Northerners began to co-opt the fundamental rights reading of the comity clause in favor of the rights of free blacks and abolitionists.[22] Yet, as Chapter 4 explores in more depth, many of the arguments made by Northerners in favor of free blacks and abolitionists were consistent with the nondiscrimination reading of the clause.[23] Put simply, although some Americans began to reimagine the privileges and immunities clause of the original Constitution in terms of fundamental rights, the evidence is overwhelmingly in the other direction. It was a nondiscrimination provision: whatever privileges and immunities a state accorded its own citizens it had to accord to citizens of sister states.

CESSION TREATIES, NATURALIZATION ACTS, AND STATE CONSTITUTIONS

There are many other uses of the phrase "privileges and immunities" in antebellum law relevant to the privileges or immunities clause of the Fourteenth Amendment, and these, too, involved nondiscrimination provisions. Three such uses are found in U.S. cession treaties, in federal naturalization acts, and in state constitutions.

Kurt Lash, in his book on the Fourteenth Amendment, draws attention to U.S. treaties of cession.[24] These treaties "promised the inhabitants of newly acquired territory that, once they were fully admitted into the Union, they would enjoy all of the privileges and immunities of US citizens." Lash quotes prominently from the Louisiana Purchase Treaty – "one of the earliest and most consistently referred to examples of national rights in antebellum America" – which provided:

> The inhabitants of the ceded territory shall be incorporated in the Union of the United States, and admitted as soon as possible, according to the principles of the Federal constitution, to the enjoyment of all the rights, advantages and immunities of citizens of the United States; and in the mean time they shall be maintained and protected in the free enjoyment of their liberty, property, and the religion which they profess.[25]

Similar clauses were included in the treaty acquiring Florida,[26] the Treaty of Guadalupe Hidalgo,[27] and the 1867 treaty ceding Alaska to the United States.[28]

Lash argues that these treaties demonstrate that the term "privileges or immunities of citizens of the United States" was a term of art that referred only to the privileges and immunities of national citizenship – a necessary component of his argument that the privileges or immunities clause of the Fourteenth Amendment incorporates the Bill of Rights against the states. We will explore Lash's claim in more depth in Chapter 6. But even now we can see that Lash may be misreading these provisions. They were not intended to define a particular set of privileges and immunities. They were, instead, standard nondiscrimination provisions routinely included when a new people was brought into a polity – as when the Welsh, the Scots, or the American colonists became or were confirmed as English citizens. These treaties provided, simply put, that whatever privileges and immunities are enjoyed by citizens of the United States – whether based in the Constitution *or* in federal statute law or common law – will be enjoyed by the citizens of newly admitted states.

In various naturalization acts, Congress also guaranteed newly naturalized citizens the same privileges and immunities as existing citizens. For example, in 1804, as Christopher Green has written, "Congress provided that upon taking citizenship oaths, surviving family members of qualified aliens who died before formal naturalization 'shall be considered as citizens of the United States, and shall be entitled to all rights and privileges as such.' "[29] In 1839, Congress declared that members of a particular Native American tribe would be "citizens of the United States to all intents and purposes" and "entitled to all the rights, privileges, and immunities of such citizens" – language repeated four years later for another tribe.[30] As Green notes, these statutes and the congressional naturalization power would be remembered by key members of the Congress that drafted the Civil Rights Act of 1866 and the Fourteenth Amendment.[31] These statutes were fundamentally about nondiscrimination. Whatever rights existing U.S. citizens had, new citizens would have also.

Finally, state constitutions also had privileges and immunities provisions that guaranteed equality among a state's own citizens. An Indiana constitutional provision declared that the legislature "shall not grant to any citizen, or class of citizens, privileges or immunities which, upon the same terms, shall not equally belong to all citizens."[32]

The Oregon constitution of 1857 similarly provided, "No law shall be passed granting to any citizen or class of citizens privileges, or immunities, which, upon the same terms, shall not equally belong to all citizens."[33] The Iowa constitution of that same year provided, "All laws of a general nature shall have a uniform operation; the General Assembly shall not grant to any citizen, or class of citizens, privileges or immunities, which, upon the same terms shall not equally belong to all citizens."[34]

None of this yet proves, of course, that the Fourteenth Amendment's privileges or immunities clause is also an antidiscrimination provision. That provision declares that no state shall make or enforce any law which shall "abridge" the privileges or immunities of citizens of the United States. But we are only at the beginning of our story. As we shall see in Chapter 4, the discrimination against the newly freed people was likely the target of the privileges or immunities clause. Indeed, the term "abridge" appears to have meant treating one group unequally when compared with another. For now, however, it is enough to understand that when the terms "privileges and immunities" appeared in state or federal constitutional discourse, they had to do with equality.

THE SCOPE OF PROTECTED PRIVILEGES AND IMMUNITIES

We have seen that privileges and immunities provisions in antebellum law were generally nondiscrimination provisions. Because the violation of the comity clause rights of free blacks was a critical issue before the Civil War, it is important to consider the scope of the privileges and immunities protected by the comity clause. Although a state, under the comity clause, had to accord the citizens of sister states the same privileges and immunities it granted its own citizens, this did not mean a state had to extend all of the rights it gave its own citizens to those of a sister state. For example, surely it need not have granted a visitor from another state the right to vote in its elections or to receive monies as a public charge for the duration of his visit? But what were the limits on the privileges and immunities that a state had to extend to the citizens of other states on an equal basis?

There were at least three approaches to this question in antebellum law. The first might be described as the "fundamental rights" approach, advanced by Justice Bushrod Washington – George Washington's nephew and inheritor of his papers and much of his estate – in the famous case of *Corfield v. Coryell*.[35] The second was articulated by Justice Benjamin Curtis in his dissent in *Dred Scott v. Sandford*,[36] in which he argued that the privileges and immunities covered by Article IV were only those that a state extended on the basis of "mere naked citizenship," without any other qualifications. The third and predominant approach was that the clause extended to all (not merely fundamental) civil rights – although it did not extend to political rights such as voting or holding office nor to the common property of a state. This was the approach that predominated at the time of Reconstruction, and indeed it was the most sensible one.

Corfield

The question in *Corfield v. Coryell*, decided in 1825[37] by Justice Washington when he was riding circuit, was whether a New Jersey law that permitted only its own citizens to collect oysters in New Jersey waters was valid under the comity clause of Article IV. Some Pennsylvania residents took a boat down the Delaware River into New Jersey waters to collect some of these oysters, and their boat was seized and they were fined ten dollars. They sought to recover their boat and the fine, arguing that the New Jersey law violated the comity clause.

Justice Washington held that the privileges and immunities of citizenship that a state had to accord to citizens of other states did not extend to the collecting of oysters. In a famous paragraph, he made the following observation:

> We feel no hesitation in confining these expressions [the privileges and immunities referenced in Article IV] to those privileges and immunities which are, in their nature, fundamental; which belong, of right, to the citizens of all free governments ... What these fundamental principles are, it would perhaps be more tedious than difficult to enumerate. They may, however, be all comprehended under the following general heads: Protection by the government; the enjoyment of life and liberty, with the right to acquire

and possess property of every kind, and to pursue and obtain happiness and safety; subject nevertheless to such restraints as the government may justly prescribe for the general good of the whole. The right of a citizen of one state to pass through, or to reside in any other state, for purposes of trade, agriculture, professional pursuits, or otherwise; to claim the benefit of the writ of habeas corpus; to institute and maintain actions of any kind in the courts of the state; to take, hold and dispose of property, either real or personal; and an exemption from higher taxes or impositions than are paid by the other citizens of the state; may be mentioned as some of the particular privileges and immunities of citizens, which are clearly embraced by the general description of privileges deemed to be fundamental . . . [38]

Justice Washington went on to suggest that perhaps other privileges and immunities "may be added," including "the elective franchise, as regulated and established by the laws or constitution of the state in which it is to be exercised."[39]

Putting aside for now Washington's reference to the political right of voting, he excluded the collecting of oysters. Article IV does not require that all the rights given to residents of a particular state must extend to citizens of other states, "much less, that in regulating the use of the common property of the citizens of such state," is the state "bound to extend to the citizens of all the other states the same advantages." Fisheries are the "common right" of all in a state, whose residents "may be considered as tenants in common of this property," exclusively entitled to use it.[40]

The upshot of this approach is that a state need not grant the citizens of other states all of the privileges it grants its own citizens; it need grant them only the *fundamental* rights of citizenship. These fundamental rights included the right to the protection of the laws ("[p]rotection by the government"), presumably due process (the "enjoyment of life and liberty"), and the right to acquire and possess property and to engage in business and lawful trade. It included other key liberty-protecting provisions in state constitutions such as those guaranteeing the writ of habeas corpus. Collecting oysters did not count as fundamental because oysters were the common property of the state itself – a scarce resource that the state could reserve for its own citizens.

Dred Scott

Justice Washington's approach in *Corfield* thus restricted the scope of the comity clause to fundamental rights. In *Dred Scott v. Sandford*, which we shall encounter in more depth in Chapter 4, Justice Curtis's dissent provided an even more restrictive account of the privileges and immunities protected by the comity clause. In that case, the Supreme Court held that Dred Scott, even if he were a free black citizen under the laws of Missouri, was not a "citizen of the United States" such that he was entitled to the benefits of the comity clause, or to the benefits of any other right in the Constitution, such as the right of citizens to sue in diversity. Part of the policy argument presented to the Court was that if free blacks were entitled to the various rights in the Constitution, including the benefit of the comity clause, then states would have to extend to the free black citizens of other states all sorts of rights that even the most radical of Republicans were not prepared to give them. These included political rights such as the right to vote – a right that Justice Washington suggested might be protected by the comity clause.

Justice Curtis responded to this argument in his dissent. Curtis argued that the rights protected by the comity clause did not include political rights, but only those rights that belonged to "mere naked citizenship." In other words, Curtis argued that the rights protected by the clause extended only to those rights that every citizen of whatever age, sex, or other condition enjoyed. This reading would have greatly restricted the scope of the clause because only a rather small subset of rights was enjoyed by all citizens of whatever age and sex. All citizens (and indeed persons) would be entitled to protection of the laws and due process, but women and children had different contract and property rights.

In support of this position, Curtis explained that there are citizens "who [are] not entitled to enjoy all the privileges and franchises which are conferred on any citizen." For example, a naturalized citizen could never be president of the United States and could not be a senator until at least nine years after his naturalization, yet a naturalized citizen was still a citizen. In all of the states, Curtis wrote, "numerous persons, though citizens, cannot vote, or cannot hold office, either on account of their age, or sex, or the want of the necessary legal qualifications."[41] Put another way, women were citizens even though in many places they could not vote, naturalized persons were citizens even though they could never become president, and so on.

Curtis argued that therefore the rights protected by the comity clause were those that each and every citizen of a particular state shared – that is, those that belonged "to citizenship" as opposed to particular citizens "attended by other qualifications." The "[p]rivileges and immunities which belong to certain citizens of a State, by reason of the operation of causes other than mere citizenship, are not conferred," Curtis wrote. And it was up to the states to decide what particular privileges and immunities should attach to "mere naked citizenship," which could then "be claimed by every citizen of each State by force of the Constitution."[42]

This reading of the privileges and immunities covered by the comity clause would certainly resolve the problem of Justice Washington's formulation, which might have extended to political rights; as explained, however, it would also greatly constrict what a state had to accord the free citizens of other states. After all, not many of the privileges and immunities listed by Justice Washington were truly conferred by "mere naked citizenship," unattended by other qualifications. Even today, very few rights are conferred by "mere naked citizenship." Most civil rights cannot be exercised by infants, many at the time could not be exercised by married women without the authority of their husbands, and so on.

Under Curtis's view, in short, there would not have been much separating a noncitizen from a citizen. Even noncitizens were entitled to the protection of the laws and due process and the like. The advantages of citizenship included, for example, the ability to acquire and possess property or to enter into certain kinds of contracts, but most infants did not have the same legal rights as adults in these matters and so these privileges of citizenship would not qualify for protection under Curtis's view of the comity clause. There is another reason why Curtis's approach seems flawed. Presumably it is a privilege of citizenship that, upon the *attainment* of "other qualifications," one becomes entitled to the particular privileges flowing from those qualifications. A rich citizen may not have the same right as a poor citizen to claim the benefits of the poor laws, but, upon becoming poor, it is a privilege of even the formerly rich to receive the benefits of such laws.

The two tests articulated by Justices Washington and Curtis, in summary, were potentially flawed in their different ways. Justice Washington's approach might have been too broad if it included political rights. But Justice Curtis's approach was too restrictive, implausibly excluding many civil rights such as property and contract rights that we ordinarily associate with the privileges of citizenship.

All Civil (but not Political) Rights

The better test, it seems, was stated by Justice Joseph Story in his influential *Commentaries on the Constitution of the United States.*[43] Article IV was intended "to confer on [the citizens of each state], if one may so say, a general citizenship; and to communicate all the privileges and immunities, which the citizens of the same state would be entitled to under the *like circumstances.*"[44] Chancellor James Kent's commentaries articulated a similar view: if citizens "remove from one state to another, they are entitled to the privileges that persons of the *same description* are entitled to in the state to which the removal is made, and to none other."[45] The right to acquire property may not be a privilege of "mere naked citizenship" if married women could not so acquire, but an unmarried female citizen of another state has the right to acquire property on the same conditions as the other unmarried female citizens of the state in which she is traveling or residing.

If Justice Story and Chancellor Kent were right, then the privileges and immunities protected by the comity clause include not merely fundamental rights nor merely those rights conferred by mere naked citizenship, but all civil rights enjoyed by citizens of the particular state under "like circumstances," exclusive perhaps of the "common property" of the state as a whole.

But what about political rights? Recall that Justice Washington suggested in *Corfield* that the right to vote might be a fundamental privilege to which Article IV extends. Yet that view seems mistaken. If a visitor from Pennsylvania were to travel through New Jersey on an election day, must New Jersey allow him to vote? That cannot be right. There is something about being a member of the particular polity that would seem to allow the citizens of a particular state to exclude outsiders from participating in the political decisions of that state. There is a big difference between civil rights and political rights. On the one hand, civil rights are the kind of rights we had in the state of nature – to exercise liberty and to acquire and possess property – as modified by those rules of civil society made to ensure no interference with the rights of others. Political rights, on the other hand, can exist only as part of a political community.

This distinction between civil and political rights was, indeed, the line drawn by most antebellum courts. In 1797, the Maryland General Court "agreed" that Article IV does not extend to "the right of election, the right of holding offices, the right of being elected," but only to personal rights, such as the right to acquire property.[46] In 1817, a Delaware court observed that "[t]he Constitution certainly meant to place, in every state, the citizens of all the states upon an equality as to their private rights, but not as to political rights."[47] The court continued:

> As long as he remains a citizen of another state, he cannot enjoy the right of suffrage nor be elected to a seat in the legislature; because these are privileges which can be exercised in one state only, and by those only who are bound by the same political compact and are obliged to support the government and to contribute with his purse and person to the exigencies of the state.[48]

In 1827, the Massachusetts Supreme Court held that the privileges conferred by Article IV on citizens are "qualified and not absolute, for [the citizens of other states] cannot enjoy the right of suffrage or of eligibility to office, without such term of residence as shall be prescribed by the constitution and laws of the State into which they shall remove."[49] In short, they did not extend to "the exercise of political or municipal rights."[50] The distinction between civil and political rights was so ingrained in antebellum law that Attorney General Caleb Cushing, in an opinion interpreting an 1855 statute guaranteeing the Choctaw and Chickasaw tribe members "all the rights, privileges, and immunities" within each other's tribal jurisdictions,[51] observed that "the distinction between *citizen* and *elector* pervades our public law."[52]

In sum, by the eve of the Civil War, although there was some variety of views as to the scope of the privileges and immunities protected by the comity clause, the general understanding was that they extended to civil rights generally, although not to political rights, and not to the common property or common rights of the state as a whole. Kurt Lash helpfully collects many of these cases and summarizes that, at least prior to *Corfield v. Coryell*, "almost every court to consider the issue adopted the same reading of Article IV." According to this reading, the "Privileges and Immunities Clause secured to sojourning state citizens equal access to a limited set of state-conferred rights," but "[t]hese rights did not include political rights such as suffrage, and they excluded any liberty not granted by the state to its own citizens."[53] The distinction between civil and political rights was widely shared in 1866, including by those who would draft the Fourteenth Amendment.[54]

PRIVILEGES AND IMMUNITIES IN STATE CONSTITUTIONS

Something that is rarely discussed in the relevant literature on the comity clause or the privileges or immunities clause of the Fourteenth Amendment is the scope of state *constitutional* rights that would have been covered by the privileges and immunities clause of Article IV. Although rarely mentioned, these state constitutional privileges and immunities will be crucial to understanding the later debate over the incorporation of the Bill of Rights against the states. Indeed if, as I shall argue later, the best original meaning of the privileges or immunities clause of the Fourteenth Amendment is that it is an antidiscrimination provision with respect to state-defined rights and a state's own citizens (much like the privileges *and* immunities clause of Article IV is an antidiscrimination provision with respect to such rights and the citizens of *other* states), then that changes the entire nature of the incorporation debate. On this reading, *if* a state grants its citizens the privilege of keeping and bearing arms, for example, then it must extend that privilege equally to all of its citizens. But the state would remain free to abolish this right as a matter of federal constitutional law.

The scope of state constitutional rights is thus of particular interest. If states largely guaranteed the same rights in the federal Bill of Rights as a matter of state constitutional law, then there would have been little need to incorporate the Bill of Rights because the states themselves would have already provided such rights. An examination of state constitutional provisions prior to the Civil War demonstrates that the state governments protected in their own constitutions, as privileges and immunities of state citizenship, almost all of the guarantees of the federal Bill of Rights. We are getting ahead of ourselves a bit, so for now let us settle for showing that the "privileges and immunities" of citizenship that would have been covered by the comity clause included a number of state constitutional rights with analogs in the federal Bill of Rights.

Thomas Cooley's 1868 treatise discusses the several constitutional protections in the state constitutions and their parallels in the federal constitution.[55] When discussing the common-law right to be secure against unreasonable searches and seizures, Cooley observes that "it has not been deemed unwise to repeat in the State constitutions, as well as in the national, the principles already settled in the common law upon this vital point in civil liberty."[56] He proceeds to describe dozens of state-level cases interpreting state constitutional law on this point.[57] On the Third Amendment provision that "no soldier shall in time of peace be quartered in any house without the consent of the owner, nor in time of war but in a manner to be prescribed by law," Cooley notes that this provision is "incorporated in the constitution of nearly every State."[58]

As for criminal accusations by grand jury indictment, "this process is still retained in most of the States, while others have substituted in its stead an information filed by the prosecuting officer of the State"; the "mode of trial," however, "is the same in all; and this is a trial by jury, surrounded by certain safeguards which are understood to be a part of the system, and which the government cannot dispense with."[59] "Wherever bail is allowed, *unreasonable bail* is not to be required . . ."[60] "The presumption of innocence is an absolute protection," and it is "required that the trial be *speedy*."[61] It is "requisite that the trial be *public*," and "[t]he defendant is entitled to be confronted with the witnesses against him."[62] The accused "shall not be twice put in

jeopardy upon the same charge."[63] "It is also a constitutional requirement that excessive fines shall not be imposed, nor cruel and unusual
punishments inflicted."[64] "With us it is a universal principle of constitutional law, that the prisoner shall be allowed a defence by counsel."[65]
Finally, "[t]he State constitutions recognize the writ of *habeas corpus*."[66]

The first of the state constitutional rights that Cooley discusses that
we would associate with the First Amendment is the right of assembly
and petition. He does not cite any specific state constitutional provisions,
but says that these rights "result[] from the very nature of [the] structure
and institutions [of republican government]."[67] Nor does Cooley cite the
various state constitutional provisions protecting the right to bear arms,
observing that "[a]mong the other defences to personal liberty should be
mentioned the right of the people to keep and bear arms."[68]

In Cooley's chapter on due process of law, he does quote every state
constitutional guarantee. "In some form of words it is to be found in
each of the State constitutions," writes Cooley, although he concedes
that he could not find an explicit due process provision among three of
the state constitutions.[69] As for the First Amendment guarantee "that
Congress shall make no law abridging the freedom of speech or of the
press," which "is almost universally regarded a sacred right, essential to
the existence and perpetuity of free government," Cooley observes that
"a provision of similar import has been embodied in each of the State
constitutions, and a constitutional principle is thereby established
which is supposed to form a shield of protection to the free expression
of opinion in every part of our land."[70]

As for religion, "[h]e who shall examine with care the American
constitutions will find nothing more fully or more plainly expressed
than the desire of their framers to preserve and perpetuate religious
liberty, and to guard against the slightest approach towards inequality
of civil or political rights based upon difference of religious belief."[71]
"Those things which are not lawful under *any* of the American constitutions" include "[a]ny law respecting an establishment of religion,"
"[c]ompulsory support, by taxation or otherwise, of religious instruc-
tion," "[c]ompulsory attendance upon religious worship," "[r]estraints
upon the free exercise of religion according to the dictates of the
conscience," and "[r]estraints upon the expression of religious
belief."[72]

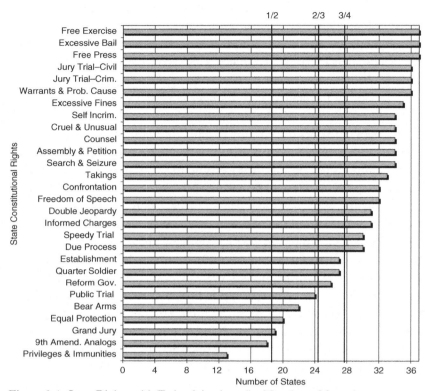

Figure 3.1 State Rights with Federal Analogs (by Number of States)

As for eminent domain, it appears that, in 1868, thirty-three of thirty-seven states had their own constitutional guarantees for takings, covering 91 percent of the American population.[73]

For present purposes, it is enough to observe that, as part of the privileges and immunities of citizenship, most states already guaranteed most federal constitutional rights as a matter of state constitutional law. These are privileges and immunities they would have had to give citizens from other states traveling or residing in their own states.

Steven Calabresi and Sarah Agudo have helpfully compiled a list of the state constitutional guarantees with federal analogs in 1868 (see Figure 3.1).[74] Although not all states guaranteed all of the same rights found in the federal Bill of Rights, most of them did secure most federal constitutional protections as a matter of their own law. As I have suggested, this will become important later on in relation to the debate over incorporation. Indeed, free press was guaranteed by *all* of the state constitutions – even though a key issue that troubled the Republican Party was the infringement of the free press rights of abolitionists.

In summary, the "privileges and immunities" provisions in antebellum law will be of great importance to understanding the Fourteenth Amendment's privileges or immunities clause. The key for present purposes is to see that these provisions were largely about equality. None defined the exact contours of a citizen's privileges and immunities. The provisions were deployed to ensure that privileges and immunities – whatever they happened to be, exclusive of political rights and the common property of the state – were granted on equal terms to all citizens. This equality requirement would become crucially important in light of the discrimination encountered by free black citizens after the Civil War – one of the very problems the Fourteenth Amendment was intended to resolve.

PART II

From Abridgment to War and Ratification

4 ABRIDGMENT OF RIGHTS BEFORE AND AFTER THE CIVIL WAR

In the first three chapters, we explored the historical legal concepts "due process of law," "protection of the laws," and "privileges and immunities" of citizenship. We are now ready to embark upon the second part of our story: the historical problem that the Fourteenth Amendment was framed to solve. As this chapter will show, that problem comprised three major issues. First, before the Civil War, there was a raging debate over the status of free black citizens of Northern states. If they were free citizens, were they not entitled under the comity clause to all of the privileges and immunities of another state's citizens when traveling through that state? To get around this apparent constitutional requirement, the Southern states, over the vigorous dissents of several Northern ones, began to argue that these free black citizens were not "citizens of the United States" within the meaning of the Constitution and thus were not entitled to the benefits of the comity clause. That, indeed, is part of what the infamous case *Dred Scott v. Sandford*[1] held: that free blacks were not, and never could be, "citizens of the United States" within the meaning of the Constitution and entitled to all of the privileges and immunities of federal citizenship.

After the Civil War, the country faced the problem of free black citizens *within* the states that had previously had slavery. Not only had these states been discriminating against the free black citizens of other states, but also now they began discriminating against the free black citizens of their *own* states – denying them, in the infamous Black Codes, the same privileges and immunities they accorded white citizens. I shall argue that the first two clauses of the Fourteenth Amendment – declaring that all persons born or naturalized in the United States are "citizens of the United States and of the State wherein they reside," and providing that "[n]o State shall make or enforce any law which shall abridge the privileges or immunities of citizens of the United States" – were principally intended to solve these two problems.

What is more, both before and after the Civil War many state governments were denying the protection of the laws not only to free and enslaved blacks, but also to those who were seeking to ameliorate their condition – the abolitionists and, later, the Unionists. Lynchings of abolitionists and free black citizens were notorious in both the North and South and were the subject of Abraham Lincoln's famous Lyceum Address. And, of course, through this denial of equal protection, many governments permitted the deprivation of life, liberty, and property without due process of law – even authorizing judicial proceedings that would be systematically unfair to black citizens.

The historical legal meanings of the concepts deployed by the Fourteenth Amendment's first section, against the backdrop of these historical problems, should make clear beyond any doubt that the Fourteenth Amendment's terms were intended to address and solve them. That they do so almost precisely suggests that the meanings of the terms in the Fourteenth Amendment's first section are what they had been in antebellum law.

ANTEBELLUM ABRIDGMENT OF INTERSTATE COMITY RIGHTS

One of the major constitutional problems in the antebellum period centered on the status of free black citizens under the comity clause of Article IV. If the clause meant what the New York court said it did in *Lemmon v. People*[2] or Justice Washington said in *Corfield v. Coryell,*[3] and if free blacks were citizens of certain states, then those free black citizens ought to have been entitled to all of the privileges and immunities of citizens in other states. That was something that Southern state governments – and some Northern ones, too – could not brook. The dispute over the constitutional status of free blacks flared up over four prominent controversies in the antebellum period: the second Missouri controversy, the Seamen Acts requiring the imprisonment of free black seamen, the Crandall affair in Connecticut, and the Supreme Court's decision in *Dred Scott*.

The Second Missouri Controversy

One of the first significant volleys in this dispute was the *second* Missouri controversy. In the first Missouri Compromise, Congress admitted Missouri as a slave state, Maine as a free state, and prohibited slavery anywhere north of the 36° 30′ parallel (with the exception of Missouri itself). When Missouri subsequently submitted its proposed constitution to Congress, it contained a provision requiring the state legislature to "pass such laws as may be necessary . . . to prevent free negroes and mulattoes from coming to and settling in this State, under any pretext whatsoever."[4]

The committee report on the admission of Missouri was issued on November 23, 1820, and noted that the committee was aware that this provision of the Missouri constitution "has been construed to apply to such of that class *as are citizens of the United States*; and that their exclusion has been deemed repugnant to the Federal Constitution."[5] On December 6, Representative Lowndes, the head of the committee, observed that "a very large majority of the free blacks in the United States were not considered citizens in their respective States," and therefore Article IV should be understood as maintaining an exception for free blacks.[6] Northern representatives argued, however, that the clause in the proposed state constitution was unconstitutional under Article IV.

Representative Sergeant argued that several states had free persons of color as citizens, and they were clearly covered by Article IV of the Constitution.[7] It is the operation of the comity clause, said Representative Storrs, "which reduces us to a perfect equality of rights with those around us, wheresoever we may transfer ourselves in every part of the Republic."[8] It was up to the states to confer "upon all the various classes of persons within their respective State jurisdictions, such rights and privileges as to themselves shall appear most conducive to their interest"; it was not up to the individual states to pick and choose which citizens of another state it would recognize as such citizens.[9] Further, Storrs added, free black seamen were considered "citizens of the United States" under a federal law protecting them from impressment.[10] The conclusion is inevitable, Storrs argued, that "[t]he citizens of the other States must enjoy within her jurisdiction all the rights, privileges, and immunities of citizens, subject to no restraints or conditions not equally imposed upon the citizens of Missouri herself."[11] If the "arbitrary" distinction in the state's constitution between free black citizens and free white citizens can be maintained, then any other arbitrary distinction among citizens could be maintained.[12]

Southern representatives disagreed, arguing that free blacks were not citizens within the meaning of the comity clause. Representative Barbour of Virginia argued that "the opponents of Missouri" must show "that those people whom she proposes to exclude are citizens, in the sense of the Constitution of the United States."[13] Because they did not enjoy all of the same civil rights as white men under like circumstances in any state, they could not be considered citizens.[14] In words similar to those the Supreme Court would use later in *Dred Scott*, Barbour argued that the Constitution was framed by the "European descendants of white men," with a "view to the liberty and rights of white men."[15] He concluded that free blacks "are not citizens in the sense of the term in which it is employed in the Constitution of the United States."[16]

Representative Smyth of Virginia similarly argued that one is a citizen only if possessed of *all* of the privileges and immunities of citizenship.[17] "He who possesses these capacities is a citizen of the United States, within the meaning of the clause of the Constitution under consideration; and he who does not possess these capacities is not."[18] "[C]an it be tolerated that the master of a negro slave should have power to make him a citizen of the United States, entitled to all the privileges of citizens in the several States?"[19]

Other Northern representatives chimed in, arguing once more that free blacks *were* citizens of the United States. "I am constrained to believe," said Representative Strong of New York, that "free negroes and mulattoes are ... citizens of the United States, and, as such, have a right peaceably to pass through, or reside in, any part of the United States."[20] Representative Hemphill agreed that the whole dispute "involves but this single inquiry – Are free negroes and mulattoes, or any of them, citizens of the United States?"[21] He believed they were.[22] Representative Eustis of Massachusetts explained that those contending that the Missouri provision was not repugnant to the Constitution "ground themselves on the [in his view, erroneous] position that blacks and mulattoes are not citizens of the United States."[23]

Charles Pinckney of South Carolina, who had been in the Constitutional Convention, falsely claimed that he had authored the comity clause in Convention and maintained that it was never intended that blacks should come within its protection: "[T]here did not then exist such a thing in the Union as a black or colored citizen, nor could I then have conceived it possible such a thing could ever have existed in it; nor, notwithstanding all that is said on the subject, do I now believe one does exist in it . . . "[24] Representative Brown of Kentucky stated the Southern position when he declared that "we have denied that free negroes and mulattoes are citizens of the United States."[25]

In the end, the second Missouri controversy ended unsatisfactorily. Henry Clay drafted a resolution that provided as a "fundamental condition" of Missouri's admission that the clause in question should not be construed to authorize the passage of any law that denied to citizens of any state any privileges and immunities to which the Constitution entitled them – thus sidestepping the whole question of precisely to what free blacks were entitled.[26]

Several Northern states, it should be observed, had similar odious laws all the way up to the eve of the Civil War.[27] In 1851, for example, Indiana's constitution provided that "[n]o negro or mulatto shall come into or settle in the State, after the adoption of this Constitution."[28] In a report on the laws of Ohio, the Ohio Anti-Slavery Convention in 1835 detailed a series of antiblack laws that prohibited the immigration into the state of free blacks unless, within twenty days of their arrival, they entered into a bond "with two or more freehold sureties, in the penal sum of five hundred dollars." The law also made it a crime to employ any such free black who had not entered into such bonds. The law effectively made it impossible for free blacks to come to Ohio to find work and support themselves.[29]

The report of the Convention observed in these laws "complete inconsistency with the fundamental principles of our government" – particularly with the comity clause of Article IV of the U.S. Constitution. The report admitted that the question of who was a citizen "admits of some doubt." But, the Convention argued, the Constitution's reference in the apportionment clauses to "free persons" and the fact that "*freemen* are considered citizens in other countries" suggests that "all *free* persons born in and residents of the United States ... are citizens, and as such, are entitled, in every state to all the privileges and immunities of citizens of these states."[30]

The report further observed that the laws of Ohio permitted deprivations of liberty and property without due process and a denial of the protection of the laws even once a free black individual was able to acquire sufficient resources for the bonds. This was a result of the laws that prohibited any black person from testifying in any action in court in which a white person was a party.[31] The report argued this provision was unconstitutional under Ohio's state constitutional provision guaranteeing access to courts and providing that "every person, for any injury done him, ... shall have remedy by the due course of law, and right and justice administered without denial or delay."[32] Here was an explicit connection of the antiblack laws to both due process and the provision in Magna Carta tied to the protection of the laws.

In 1859, John Bingham, the principal author of the Fourteenth Amendment's first section, rose in Congress to oppose Oregon's proposed constitution, which provided that "[n]o free negro or mulatto, not residing in this State at the time of the adoption of this constitution, shall ever come, reside or be, within this State, or hold any real estate, or make any contract, or maintain any suit therein."[33] Bingham argued that this provision violated the comity clause of Article IV because free blacks were "citizens of the United States, and as such are entitled to all the privileges and immunities of citizens of the United States."[34] Bingham did not mean to say that free blacks were entitled to the same *political* rights in Oregon as whites. If the people of Oregon saw fit, they could even exclude from political rights "the best portion of the citizens of the United States": the "free intelligent women of the land." But what they could *not* deny to these black individuals, or to women, was the equality "to the right to live; to the right to know; to argue and to utter, according to conscience; to work and enjoy the product of their toil."[35]

Here, merely a few years before the adoption of the Fourteenth Amendment, its principal author was explaining that prohibitions on free blacks like that at issue in the second Missouri controversy still existed and still violated the comity clause because such free blacks were "citizens of the United States" within the meaning of the Constitution.

Seamen Acts

The dispute over the constitutional status of free blacks flared up after the Vesey plot in South Carolina in 1821–22. This alleged slave uprising, led by a free black, Denmark Vesey of Charleston, was perhaps more imagined than real. As William Wiecek explains, these black individuals "had actually done nothing; none were caught with weapons; none were taken under incriminating circumstances."[36] Nevertheless, three dozen alleged conspirators were hanged after proceedings in specialized slave courts.

Putting aside the due process problems with such proceedings, what concerns us here is specifically the aftermath. After the plot, South Carolinians observed that Vesey and a few conspirators had been seamen or slaves of shipyard owners. They therefore concluded "that free black seamen coming into Charleston on shore leave who mingled with free and enslaved blacks contaminated Carolina's slaves."[37] South Carolina thus enacted the Negro Seamen's Act of 1822, which provided for the jailing of all free black seamen whose vessels came into Charleston until their vessels cleared, at the expense of the vessel's owner; if the vessel's owner failed to redeem the sailor, the sailor was to be sold into slavery.[38]

President John Quincy Adams argued that this statute was unconstitutional. His attorney general, William Wirt, wrote an opinion declaring the statute to be an unconstitutional interference with commerce.[39] The response in the South, Wiecek explains, was explosive.[40] In 1829, 1830, and 1832, three other Southern states followed suit with their own acts providing for the imprisoning of free black seamen. Proslavery Andrew Jackson was then in the White House, and his attorney general, John Berrien, reversed Wirt's earlier opinion.[41] Berrien's successor the next year – Roger B. Taney – affirmed Berrien's position in an opinion never formally published and added an argument that he would repeat a quarter-century later as Chief Justice of the United States: blacks "were not looked upon as citizens by the contracting parties who formed the Constitution" and "were evidently not supposed to be included by the term *citizens*."[42]

The controversy continued, and when John Quincy Adams was again a member of the House of Representatives in 1843, he introduced into the House a remonstrance by Boston merchants arguing that the various Seamen Acts violated the comity clause of Article IV. A select committee in the House agreed, reporting as follows:

> The committee have no hesitation in agreeing with the memorialists, that the acts of which they complain, are violations of the privileges of citizenship guarantied by the Constitution of the United States. The Constitution of the United States expressly provides, (art. 4, sec. 2) that "citizens of each State shall be entitled to all privileges and immunities of citizens in the several States." Now, it is well understood that some of the States of this Union recognise no distinction of color in relation to citizenship. Their citizens are all free; their freemen all citizens. In Massachusetts, certainly – the State from which this memorial emanates – the colored man has enjoyed the full and equal privileges of citizenship since the last remnant of slavery was abolished within her borders by the constitution of 1780, nine years before the adoption of the Constitution of the United States. The Constitution of the United States, therefore, at its adoption, found the colored man of Massachusetts a citizen of Massachusetts, and entitled him, as such, to all the privileges and immunities of a citizen in the several States. And of these privileges and immunities, the acts set forth in the memorial constitute a plain and palpable violation. . . . However extended or however limited may be the privileges and immunities which it secures, the citizens of each State are entitled to them equally, without discrimination of color or condition . . . [43]

In words that still resonate today, the committee rejected the "police powers" argument made by the Southern governments, observing that such a power "can never be permitted to abrogate the constitutional privileges of a whole class of citizens, upon grounds, not of any temporary, moral or physical condition, but of distinctions which originate in their birth, and which are as permanent as their being."[44] A two-man minority report disagreed with the majority report, and no action was taken.[45]

After Congress refused to take any action, Massachusetts sent Samuel Hoar to South Carolina and Henry Hubbard to Louisiana to remonstrate against the Seamen Acts. Both men were threatened with lynching, and both had to flee the respective states – neither of which would extend to them the protection of the laws.[46] The South Carolina legislature then resolved, in a statement on Hoar's mission, "[t]hat free negroes and persons of color are not citizens of the United States within the meaning of the Constitution, which confers upon the citizens of one State the privileges and immunities of citizens in the several States."[47] In 1850, when the U.S. Senate was again debating these Seamen Acts, a representative from Louisiana recalled of Hubbard's mission that a report by the legislature was made that Louisiana's laws "were not in violation of any rights given to citizens of the United States under the constitution."[48]

The Crandall Affair

In 1832, Prudence Crandall, a Quaker woman who ran a school for girls in Connecticut, admitted a black girl. Parents objected, and so Crandall chose to operate the school entirely as one for free black girls – attracting several such students from other states. The opposition was fierce, and the Connecticut legislature enacted what abolitionists referred to as the "Connecticut Black Law," requiring the permission of a town's selectmen to operate a private school for black nonresidents.[49] Crandall's first prosecution under this statute ended in a hung jury, and a second prosecution was commenced before Chief Judge Daggett of the Connecticut Supreme Court of Errors.[50] The constitutionality of the Connecticut law was called into question by Crandall's counsel, as described in the report on appeal:

> The defendant claimed, and prayed the court to instruct the jury, that if they should find these facts proved, such coloured persons were to be regarded as citizens of the states where they respectively belonged and were born; and that they were entitled to the privileges and immunities secured by the 2nd section of the 4th article of the constitution of the *United States*; and that said statute, depriving

them of the privilege of attending said school, for the purpose of acquiring useful knowledge, while the privilege of attending the same school for the same purpose, was allowed to coloured persons belonging to this state, and imposing a penalty for harbouring and boarding coloured persons not belonging to this state, while no such penalty was imposed for harbouring and boarding the coloured inhabitants of this state, was repugnant to the constitution of the *United States*, and void.[51]

Chief Judge Daggett instructed the jury that, to the contrary, the Connecticut statute was constitutional. "The plain and obvious meaning of this provision [the comity clause]," Daggett instructed, "is, to secure to the *citizens* of all the states, the same privileges as are secured to our own, by our own state laws."[52] But, Daggett urged the jury, "[t]he persons contemplated in this act are *not citizens* within the obvious meaning of that section of the constitution of the *United States*"; "[t]o my mind, it would be a perversion of terms, and the well known rule of construction, to say, that slaves, free blacks, or Indians, were citizens, within the meaning of that term, as used in the constitution."[53] Therefore Connecticut's law "is not contrary to the 2d section of the 4th art. of the constitution of the United States; for that embraces only citizens."[54] On appeal, counsel for the state asked, "Can it be entertained for one moment, that those who framed the constitution should hold one portion of *a race of men* in bondage, while the other portion were made *citizens?*"[55]

Crandall had been convicted, but the state's highest court dodged the thorny constitutional question and held that the indictment was insufficient under the statute.[56] Over thirty years later, however, at the very end of the Civil War and on the eve of the Fourteenth Amendment's drafting, one judge on the Connecticut Supreme Court recalled that the entire court, with the exception of Daggett, believed that free blacks could be citizens of the United States and that the jury charge had been incorrect.[57] Not that any of that would have mattered in 1834: After Crandall's conviction was overturned for insufficiency of the indictment, mobs in the Connecticut town tried to burn down the school. They broke the windows and terrorized the girls. Crandall had no choice but to give up and close up shop.[58]

Dred Scott v. Sandford

The culmination of these political and legal struggles over the status of free blacks was the notorious case of *Dred Scott v. Sandford*. The facts are complicated, but boil down to this: Dred Scott lived with his master for two years in Illinois, which was a free state; according to Illinois law, a sufficiently long stay there made Scott a free man. When Scott was returned to Missouri by his master's widow, he sued for his freedom in state court; under earlier Missouri precedents, the Missouri courts would have applied Illinois law as a matter of comity, and Scott would be free. The Missouri courts overturned those precedents and applied Missouri law instead, declaring that Scott was therefore still a slave. It would seem that, before the judgment became final, the widow sold Scott to her brother, Mr. Sanford (whose name is misspelled in the official report as Sandford), a citizen of New York. Thus Scott commenced a new lawsuit, this time in federal court, because Article III of the Constitution grants federal courts jurisdiction in suits between "citizens" of different states.[59]

The Supreme Court addressed whether any black person could "become a member of the political community formed and brought into existence by the Constitution of the United States, and as such become entitled to all the rights, and privileges, and immunities, guarantied by that instrument to the citizen," including the right of suing in federal court.[60] Roger Taney, now Chief Justice, held that black people "are not included, and were not intended to be included, under the word 'citizens' in the Constitution, and can therefore claim none of the rights and privileges which that instrument provides for and secures to citizens of the United States." Even if a black man were a citizen of a state, that still did not make him "a citizen of the United States" entitled to sue in court and to the comity clause rights of Article IV.[61]

Taney rested his argument on two grounds. First, Congress's power of naturalization is exclusive, and therefore states could not create new citizens and impose these citizens upon all of the other states. Second, the political community that created the Constitution did not include black people; they had "for more than a century before been regarded as beings of an inferior order" and had "no rights which the white man was bound to respect."[62]

Justice Benjamin Curtis, in dissent, utterly obliterated these arguments. As for the naturalization power, this was the power to remove the disability of alienage and to *make* new citizens. It did not include a power to remove the *already-existing* privilege of citizenship. And the Constitution assumed, in the clause declaring that only natural-born citizens could become president, that any free person born on U.S. soil was a citizen. As for the original political community, Curtis showed that, in at least five of the states prior to the adoption of the federal Constitution, free blacks "were not only citizens," but also "such of them as had the other necessary qualifications possessed the franchise of electors, on equal terms with other citizens."[63] Thus they already were citizens – and nothing in the Constitution deprived them of that citizenship.

Both Abraham Lincoln and Stephen Douglas understood the relevance of the *Dred Scott* decision to the debate over the privileges and immunities clause of Article IV. In his June 17, 1858 speech in Springfield, Illinois, Lincoln observed that the first implication of the decision was that no slave or a descendant of such slave "can ever be a citizen of any State, in the sense of that term as used in the Constitution of the United States," and that as a result they are deprived "of the benefit of that provision of the United States Constitution which declares that 'citizens of each State shall be entitled to all privileges and immunities of citizens in the several States.' "[64]

A few weeks later, in Chicago, Douglas responded:

[Mr. Lincoln] objects to [*Dred Scott*] because that decision declared that a negro descended from African parents who were brought here and sold as slaves is not, and cannot be a citizen of the United States. He says it is wrong, because it deprives the negro of the benefits of that clause of the Constitution which says that citizens of one State shall enjoy all the privileges and immunities of citizens of the several States; in other words, he thinks it wrong because it deprives the negro of the privileges, immunities, and rights of citizenship, which pertain, according to that decision, only to the white man.

I am free to say to you that in my opinion this government of ours is founded on the white basis. It was made by the white man, for the benefit of the white man, to be administered by white men, in such manner as they should determine.[65]

This exchange between Lincoln and Douglas leaves us with no doubt that the constitutional status of free blacks remained a key constitutional dispute leading up to the Civil War, as it would remain after. Whether free black citizens counted as citizens of the United States, and whether they were entitled to the same privileges and immunities as white citizens, would be a key issue the framers of the Fourteenth Amendment would seek to resolve.

THE SUPPRESSION OF CIVIL RIGHTS

An important part of our story is the infringement of civil liberty that was required to perpetuate the institution of slavery. The greatest battle over civil liberties involved speech and press, and the suppression of abolitionist literature in particular. This will become important because many proponents of incorporation of the Bill of Rights against the states claim that the framers of the Fourteenth Amendment were aware of this history and were concerned with widespread infringement of such civil liberties in the various states. As I will argue in a later chapter, this history probably does not support incorporation – but it is nevertheless important to the general background of the Fourteenth Amendment.

In the late 1820s and early 1830s, manumission societies and independent publishers engaged in "the great postal campaign" to circulate abolitionist literature throughout the United States, including in the South.[66] In 1829, a black Bostonian published *Appeal to the Colored Citizens of the World*, calling on enslaved blacks to defend themselves against their masters.[67] Soon after, William Lloyd Garrison began to publish the *Liberator*.[68] In the wake of the Missouri debate, the Vesey plot, and the various Seamen Acts, the South was not about to let such incendiary materials within its borders.

The constitutional dispute flared up in 1835 when the postmaster of Charleston, South Carolina, requested an opinion from Postmaster General Amos Kendall about whether he had to distribute abolitionist literature. Kendall's opinion was ambivalent, noting that postmasters had an "obligation to the laws," but also "to the communities in which we live," and he directed the Charleston postmaster to do whatever he thought best on the basis of "the character of the papers detained and the circumstances by which you are surrounded."[69] The issue became moot because, that same day, a mob seized and destroyed the mailings, suggesting yet further denial of the protection of the laws in the state.

Kendall subsequently sought President Andrew Jackson's views, and Jackson recommended that Congress prohibit the distribution of abolitionist literature in the South.[70] This proposal was defeated by an odd combination of Southerners led by John C. Calhoun and Northerners, on the ground that it was an abridgment of the freedom of speech *and* that it violated the states' police powers. After all, the Southerners worried, if the federal government could prohibit abolitionist literature on the ground that it was incitement to insurrection, then it could also decide that this same literature was *not* incitement – a risk the Southern governments were unwilling to take.[71] Northerners Daniel Webster and John Davis argued that not only would such a proposal abridge the freedom of speech, but also it would require unreasonable searches and seizures in violation of the Fourth Amendment.[72]

Although Congress took no action, the Southern state governments thoroughly suppressed such literature. Tennessee banned all publications "calculated to excite discontent ... amongst the slaves or free persons of color," and Maryland, Missouri, and Mississippi adopted similar prohibitions.[73] South Carolina, Georgia, Virginia, and Alabama all demanded that the *Northern* states censor antislavery publications, associations, and meetings.[74] South Carolina outdid the others, with its governor demanding that the Northern states make the distribution of abolitionist literature a capital offense.[75] Although some Northern states expressed sympathy, many rejected these suggestions; the Vermont legislature even adopted a joint resolution declaring that "neither Congress nor the state Governments have any constitutional right to abridge the free expression of opinions, or the transmission of them through the public mail."[76] In any event, such calls upon the Northern states were unnecessary, for no Southern postmaster would deliver abolitionist mails. In the South, the federal postal laws were a dead letter.[77]

The suppression of civil liberty became a central theme for many abolitionists. They observed that the perpetuation of slavery required repression generally. As the founders of the New York State Anti-Slavery Society declared in 1835, "the time has come to settle the great question whether the north shall give up its liberty to preserve slavery to the south, or whether the south shall give up its slavery to preserve liberty to the whole nation."[78] Or, as the abolitionist James Birney wrote in a letter that same year, "The contest is becoming – has become – one, not alone of freedom for the black, but of freedom for the white. . . . The antagonist principles of liberty and slavery have been roused into action and one or the other must be victorious."[79] As Professor Akhil Amar has written, "Simply put, slavery required repression. Speech and writing critical of slavery ... was incendiary and had to be suppressed."[80] The salience of the suppression of civil liberty can be seen in the 1856 slogan of the Republican Party, whose candidate for president was John C. Frémont: "Free Speech, Free Press, Free Men, Free Labor, Free Territory, and Frémont."[81]

PRIVATE VIOLENCE AND THE PROTECTION OF THE LAWS

Mob Violence before the Civil War

The proponents of slavery did not simply rest on their legislative victories; they also subjected abolitionists to mob violence. As Michael Kent Curtis has explained, "In addition to being legally restricted from spreading antislavery doctrine, abolitionists were the victims of mob violence. In these cases local authorities often failed to make any effort to protect the victims."[82] There was, in other words, a continuing denial of the protection of the laws in both the Northern and Southern states.

In reference to abolitionists, the aptly named Governor Lynch of Mississippi warned that "necessity will sometimes prompt a summary mode of trial and punishment unknown to the law."[83] One governor of South Carolina is reported to have said, "I would have those who oppose slavery, if caught in our jurisdiction, put to death without benefit of clergy."[84]

In one particularly well-known case from 1837, antiabolitionists murdered abolitionist publisher Elijah Lovejoy in Alton, Illinois, while he defended his fourth printing press from a mob (previous mobs having destroyed his first three). The city authorities had refused to provide any protection.[85] Lovejoy's situation was hardly unique.[86] Jacobus tenBroek has written that "[t]he immediate need of the abolitionists in the free states was for protection against riot, arson, assault, and murder," because "breaches of established rights were perpetrated almost daily" with the knowledge of, and often in the presence of, public officials.[87]

This history cannot be too much emphasized in light of later debates over the meaning of the Fourteenth Amendment. As we shall see, proponents of incorporation often rely on Republican and abolitionist experience with the denial of civil rights in the cause of suppressing abolitionism as supporting a general understanding that the Bill of Rights had to apply to the states. The real issue was not the general lack of civil liberties, however, but rather the failure to extend such liberties to certain groups, or the failure to provide *protection* for these known and established rights. As tenBroek writes, "Enforcement of *existing* laws rather than the passage of new laws or the repeal of old ones was [the abolitionists'] crying need."[88]

Indeed, Elijah Lovejoy himself emphasized that he was being denied protection for his known rights. When he pleaded with the citizens of Alton just days before his murder, Lovejoy did say that his free speech rights were guaranteed to him "by the constitution of my country," and here he could have meant either the constitution of the state of Illinois or the U.S. Constitution. But the bigger point was that it was never questioned that he had certain rights; rather, "the question to be decided is, whether I shall be protected in the exercise and enjoyment of those rights – *that is the question, sir;* – whether my property shall be protected, whether I shall be suffered to go home to my family at night without being assailed, and threatened with tar and feathers, and assassination."[89] Other abolitionists similarly sought to be "protected" in the "enjoyment of our civil and religious liberties."[90]

Abraham Lincoln saw this failure of government to provide the protection of the laws – and the failure of the people to abide by the republican spirit – as the cause that would directly lead to the demise of our political institutions. In his famous Lyceum Address in 1838, Lincoln warned against "the increasing disregard for law which pervades the country; the growing disposition to substitute the wild and furious passions, in lieu of the sober judgment of Courts; and the worse than savage mobs, for the executive ministers of justice."[91] Accounts of such mob rule, Lincoln said, "pervaded the country, from New England to Louisiana; – they are neither peculiar to the eternal snows of the former, nor the burning suns of the latter; – they are not the creature of climate – neither are they confined to the slave-holding, or the non-slave-holding States."[92] Of course, he must have had the Lovejoy lynching, which had occurred in neighboring Alton, fresh in mind.[93]

Lincoln described the lynchings that were occurring in Mississippi:

> In the Mississippi case, they first commenced by hanging the regular gamblers; a set of men, certainly not following for a livelihood, a very useful, or very honest occupation; but one which, so far from being forbidden by the laws, was actually licensed by an act of the Legislature, passed but a single year before. Next, negroes, suspected of conspiring to raise an insurrection, were caught up and hanged in all parts of the State: then, white men, supposed to be leagued with the negroes; and finally, strangers, from neighboring States, going thither on business, were, in many instances subjected to the same fate. Thus went on this process of hanging, from gamblers to negroes, from negroes to white citizens, and from these to strangers; till, dead men were seen literally dangling from the boughs of trees upon every road side; and in numbers almost sufficient, to rival the native Spanish moss of the country, as a drapery of the forest.[94]

And then Lincoln relayed the story of a mulatto man in St. Louis, Missouri, who "was seized in the street, dragged to the suburbs of the city, chained to a tree, and actually burned to death; and all within a single hour from the time he had been a freeman, attending to his own business, and at peace with the world."[95] "Such are the effects of mob law," said Lincoln, "and such are the scenes, becoming more and more frequent in this land so lately famed for love of law and order."[96]

What does any of this have to do with the perpetuation of our political institutions, Lincoln asked? He answered:

> When men take it in their heads to day, to hang gamblers, or burn murderers, they should recollect, that, in the confusion usually attending such transactions, they will be as likely to hang or burn some one who is neither a gambler nor a murderer as one who is; and that, acting upon the example they set, the mob of to-morrow, may, and probably will, hang or burn some of them by the very same mistake. And not only so; the innocent, those who have ever set their faces against violations of law in every shape, alike with the guilty, fall victims to the ravages of mob law; and thus it goes on, step by step, *till all the walls erected for the defence of the persons and property of individuals, are trodden down, and disregarded.*[97]

Here, Lincoln is referring to the breakdown of the protection of the laws. The mob spirit further engenders a lawless spirit and complete disregard for free government among all who participate in it – and more still good and lawful men will not long remain attached to a government when, "seeing their property destroyed; their families insulted, and their lives endangered; their persons injured; . . . [they] become tired of, and disgusted with, a Government that offers them no protection."[98] "[I]f the laws be continually despised and disregarded, if their rights to be secure in their persons and property, are held by no better tenure than the caprice of a mob," then "the alienation of their affections from the Government is the natural consequence; and to that, sooner or later, it must come."[99]

Several writers in the 1860s expressly connected mob violence to denial of the protection of the laws. Milo Bennett, a justice on the Vermont Supreme Court, wrote in 1864 that "where the premeditated object and intent of a riotous assembly is to prevent, by force and violence, the execution of the laws of the United States . . . or to deprive any class of the community of the protection afforded by law," such rioters are guilty of treason.[100] Similarly, Francis Wharton's 1868 criminal law treatise used identical language to that of Bennett and gave the examples of "burning down all churches or meeting-houses of a particular sect, under color of reforming a public grievance, or to release all prisoners in the public jails, and the like."[101]

On the other side of the Atlantic, in an 1867 collection of his writings, William Plunket wrote, "Every subject of this realm has an undoubted right to the protection of the laws – to the security of his person and his property – and still more, to the full assurance of such safety."[102] Thus assemblies "must not assemble under such circumstances, whether of numbers or otherwise, as to excite well-grounded terror in the minds of their fellow-subjects, or to disturb their tranquil and assured enjoyment of the protection of the laws, free from all reasonable apprehension of force or violence."[103]

Perhaps most poignant, however, is an article that appeared in an 1863 issue of the *National Anti-Slavery Standard* under the title "Equal Protection under the Law." As Eric Foner recently explained, the article "had to do with the failure of police to protect blacks from mob assault during the New York City Draft Riots."[104] In short, the antebellum period witnessed an epidemic of mob rule that was associated in the minds of legal and political thinkers with a denial of the protection of the laws. Mob action was directed not only at abolitionists, of course, but also at both enslaved and free blacks. More still, many abolitionists correctly argued that the institution of slavery itself was a denial of the protection of the laws. Not only did the institution routinely permit private abuses against slaves, but it also denied basic legal protections for the enslaved individual's natural rights to liberty and property, and it therefore violated the reciprocal requirement of allegiance for protection.[105]

Mob Violence after the Civil War

Mob violence and the denial of the protection of the laws became an even more prominent problem after the Civil War, right as the Thirty-Ninth Congress that was to draft the Fourteenth Amendment convened. Violence against freedmen and Unionists was rampant in the South. In the words of General Terry in Virginia, Unionists were not "secure in the enjoyment of their rights in a Secession community; they could not rely upon the State Courts for justice."[106] Senator Trumbull – a key player in reconstruction – noted that "in many parts of the South Union men, whether natives of the state or from the North, are ... now without protection to person or property except as it is afforded by the military."[107] Another Union general, soon to become a congressman from Massachusetts, argued that because "[t]he Southern man ... knows that he can go to any part of the North and speak his sentiments freely," he did not want any part of the South represented in Congress "until you and I can go and argue the principles of free government without fear of the knife or pistol, or of being murdered by a mob."[108]

Two historians have put it thus: "It was tough enough to fight against injustices resulting from positive acts. But it was far more difficult for federal officers and Negroes to combat acts and nonacts by state and local officials that permitted crimes committed by private persons to flourish."[109] Paul Finkleman has recently surveyed the voluminous testimony presented to Congress describing atrocities against the freed people and their white allies.[110] "Blacks disappeared, were beaten, maimed, and killed," all with impunity.[111]

General Grant had to take matters into his own hands, issuing a military order "protecting colored persons from prosecution" for offenses for which whites were not "prosecuted or punished in the same manner and degree,"[112] and another directing military officials to arrest all persons committing crimes, including against blacks, "in cases where the civil authorities have failed, neglected, or are unable to arrest and bring such parties to trial."[113] Grant dispatched troops to North Mississippi "to suppress outrages in that section" and to "suppress violence that is now being committed by outlawry," for which the civil authorities had failed to make arrests.[114]

This ongoing denial of the protection of the laws was a key problem that the framers of the Fourteenth Amendment would seek to resolve. The public report of the Joint Committee on Reconstruction observed that the Freedmen's Bureau was routinely obstructed, that "without its protection the colored people would not be permitted to labor at fair prices, and could hardly live in safety," that "without the protection of United States troops, Union men ... would be obliged to abandon their homes," and, further, that "the local authorities are at no pains to prevent or punish" numerous "acts of cruelty, oppression, and murder."[115]

In sum, the antebellum period witnessed the violation of the comity clause rights of free blacks, the abridgment of press and speech freedoms, and the widespread denial of the protection of the laws (and the corollary denial of due process) as a result of mob violence. These problems persisted after the war, and the framers had them in mind when drafting the Fourteenth Amendment. They also had another problem in center view: the abridgment of the privileges and immunities of free black citizens within the Southern states after abolition.

POSTBELLUM BLACK CODES AND THE ABRIDGMENT OF STATE-DEFINED RIGHTS

After the Civil War, with the end of slavery, the Southern state legislatures began to make law on the subject of their newly freed black citizens. In statutes referred to as the "Black Codes," which ostensibly conferred rights on the freedmen that they had not had before, the Southern governments sought to reduce the free blacks to a system as near to slavery as possible.[116] (As we have seen with the example of Ohio, Northern states, too, had a variety of such codes, although they were generally less harsh.[117]) Many of these Black Codes required the newly freed men and women to find employment by January of each year, and they were bound to that employment for the entire year.[118] Louisiana's statute was typical, providing that abandoning such employment would result in forfeiture of all wages earned up until the time of abandonment.[119] The statute also required a minimum number of work hours per day – namely, ten hours in the summer and nine in the winter.[120] In South Carolina, these black individuals were prohibited from following any occupation other than farmer or servant unless they were licensed and paid a tax.[121]

Vague and broad vagrancy and anti-assembling laws were enacted to ensure that police would have wide discretion to arrest unsuspecting black individuals. Mississippi's was typical. Part of the act applicable only to "freedmen, free negroes and mulattoes" provided that any such person found after the second Monday in January 1866 "without lawful employment or business, or found unlawfully assembling themselves together," would be deemed a vagrant. Any whites assembling with "freedmen, free negroes or mulattoes, on terms of equality," would also be deemed vagrants.[122]

In the various Codes, newly freed blacks were permitted to testify in court only under certain conditions, for example, when another black individual was a party or a victim.[123] Florida's statute prohibited their testimony by deposition, "otherwise than in such manner as will enable the court and jury to judge of the credibility of the witness."[124] Virginia's similarly provided against testimony by deposition and permitted blacks to be witnesses only when another black individual was a witness.[125]

Under the Codes, these newly freed people could not acquire property on the same terms as whites. Mississippi's code, for example, provided that blacks could acquire only personal and not real property.[126] Out of an abundance of caution, the statute made sure to mention that this should not be construed to allow these individuals to *rent or lease* either, "except in incorporated towns or cities" under the control of municipal authorities.[127]

Importantly, the Black Codes mostly denied blacks the right to keep and bear arms – the one right perhaps most critical to ensure their own self-defense. Florida's statute provided "[t]hat it shall not be lawful for any negro, mulatto, or other person of color to own, use, or keep in his possession, or under his control, any bowie-knife, dirk, sword, fire-arms, or ammunition of any kind, unless he first obtain a license to do so from the judge of probate of the county in which he may be a resident for the time being," which judge is authorized to issue licenses "upon the recommendation of two respectable citizens of the county, certifying to the peaceful and orderly character of the applicant."[128] Mississippi similarly prohibited any "freedman, negro, or mulatto" not in military service of the United States and not licensed by the county, to "keep or carry fire-arms of any kind, or any ammunition, dirk or bowie knife."[129]

In summarizing these Black Codes, Charles Fairman has written, "The Negro's place was made clear: he was to be a laborer, chiefly a plantation laborer, bound by the year; his wage would, in practice, be set by the employers; to be without employment would lead to severe sanctions. It was not contemplated that the Negro would progress, for the roads were barred."[130] This was the state of affairs as Congress convened to discuss Reconstruction legislation and what would eventually become the Fourteenth Amendment. "The Southern States had spoken, and the impact was felt in Congress from the moment it assembled."[131]

5 THE FOURTEENTH AMENDMENT

When the Thirty-Ninth Congress convened in December 1865, the problems of the antebellum period persisted alongside the new problem of the Black Codes. Congress sought to address these problems – the denial of the protection of the laws and the concomitant denial of due process, as well the abridgment of the privileges and immunities of black citizens – by enacting or proposing three pieces of legislation: the Civil Rights Act of 1866, the Privileges and Immunities Bill of 1866, and the Second Freedmen's Bureau Act of 1866.

In the Civil Rights Act, Congress sought to declare the newly freed blacks to be citizens of the United States entitled to the same privileges and immunities as white citizens in the various states – a direct attack on the Black Codes. The Thirty-Ninth Congress also introduced the Privileges and Immunities Bill, which sought to declare these black citizens to be entitled to all privileges and immunities under the comity clause of Article IV. It never became law, likely because of constitutional objections. In the Second Freedmen's Bureau Act, as well as in the Reconstruction Acts enacted after the Fourteenth Amendment was submitted to the states for ratification, Congress created government institutions in the South to provide physical and judicial protection to freed people and to Unionists on the ground that there was inadequate "protection" for life and property in the rebel states.

The constitutionality of each of these provisions was in doubt, and the Fourteenth Amendment was intended to provide a constitutional basis for them. It provides:

All persons born or naturalized in the United States, and subject to the jurisdiction thereof, are citizens of the United States and of the State wherein they reside. No State shall make or enforce any law which shall abridge the privileges or immunities of citizens of the United States; nor shall any State deprive any person of life, liberty, or property, without due process of law; nor deny to any person within its jurisdiction the equal protection of the laws.[1]

The fifth section of the Fourteenth Amendment adds: "Congress shall have the power to enforce, by appropriate legislation, the provisions of this article."[2]

The meaning of the Fourteenth Amendment is clear, and it is elegant. It was intended to constitutionalize each of these Acts, whose constitutionality was in doubt, by deploying birthright citizenship and each of the antebellum legal concepts discussed in Part I. It was further intended to embed these legal requirements directly in the fundamental law and insulate them against shifting popular majorities. The Amendment deploys the antebellum legal concepts, in short, to solve directly the question of black citizenship and comity rights, the discrimination of the Black Codes, and the widespread denial of due process and protection of the laws.

THE LEGISLATION OF THE RECONSTRUCTION CONGRESS

Confronted with the problem of the Black Codes, the Thirty-Ninth Congress got to work. Senator Lyman Trumbull, chair of the Senate's judiciary committee, introduced the bill that would become the Civil Rights Act of 1866.[3] The Act, which differed only slightly from the original bill, provided:

That all persons born in the United States and not subject to any foreign power, excluding Indians not taxed, are hereby declared to be citizens of the United States; *and such citizens*, of every race and color, without regard to any previous condition of slavery or involuntary servitude ... *shall have the same right*, in every State and Territory in the United States, to make and enforce contracts, to sue, be parties, and give evidence, to inherit, purchase, lease, sell, hold, and convey real and personal property, and to full and equal benefit of all laws and proceedings for the security of persons and property, *as is enjoyed by white citizens,* and shall be subject to like punishment, pains, and penalties, and to none other, any law, statute, ordinance, regulation, or custom, to the contrary notwithstanding.[4]

Trumbull was explicit that the purpose of the Act was to overturn the various Black Codes in the states: "Since the abolition of slavery, the Legislatures which have assembled in the insurrectionary States have passed laws relating to the freedmen, and in nearly all the States they have discriminated against them."[5] Trumbull declared, "They deny them certain rights, subject them to severe penalties, and still impose upon them the very restrictions which were imposed upon them in consequence of the existence of slavery, and before it was abolished."[6] The purpose of the Civil Rights Bill was "to destroy all these discriminations, and to carry into effect" the Thirteenth Amendment.[7]

What is striking about this statute is that it was merely an anti-discrimination provision. It did not dictate to the Southern governments what privileges to contract, to sue, and so forth, they had to provide to their citizens; it provided merely that whatever privileges the government accorded to "white citizens," it had also to extend to black citizens on an equal basis. Black citizens were emphatically declared to be citizens of the United States. Importantly for our later analysis of the Fourteenth Amendment's privileges or immunities clause, the Civil Rights Act describes the privileges and immunities of "citizens of the United States" as including a whole host of *state-defined* privileges and immunities.

The constitutionality of the Civil Rights Act, however, was in doubt. Many argued that Congress had no constitutional power to enact a law imposing such an equality requirement directly upon the state governments. Even Republicans had doubts: one representative from Ohio stated that it would in effect declare "that Congress has authority to go into the States and manage and legislate with regard to all the personal rights of the citizen – rights of life, liberty, and property," thereby "render[ing] this Government no longer a Government of limited powers."[8] Democrats were, of course, even more skeptical:

"Has Congress the power to enter the domain of a State, and destroy its police regulations with regard to the punishment inflicted upon negroes?"[9] Of course, the bill did not actually regulate the content of state legislation, except in a minimalist sense: it required *equality* with respect to whatever rights a state happened to extend its white citizens.

But the question remained what constitutional source of power permitted Congress to enact such legislation. President Andrew Johnson expressed this concern in his veto message:

> Hitherto, every subject embraced in the enumeration of rights contained in the bill has been considered as exclusively belonging to the States; they all relate to the internal policy and economy of the respective States. They are matters which, in each State, concern the domestic condition of its people, varying in each according to its peculiar circumstances and the safety and well-being of its own citizens. . . .
>
> [W]here can we find a Federal prohibition against the power of any State to discriminate, as do most of them, between aliens and citizens, between artificial persons called corporations, and naturalized persons, in the right to hold real estate?
>
> [. . .]
>
> [T]he details of this bill . . . interfere with the municipal legislation of the States; with relations existing exclusively between a State and its citizens, or between inhabitants of the same State; an absorption and assumption of power by the General Government which, if acquiesced in, must sap and destroy our federative system of limited power, and break down the barriers which preserve the rights of the States.[10]

The importance of Andrew Johnson's veto, Kurt Lash explains, was "obvious" at the time, and the veto "exploded across newspaper headlines throughout the United States, with many papers printing [the] accompanying message in full."[11] Republicans were unmoved, overriding the veto and enacting the bill into law by a vote of 122–41. Nevertheless, the constitutionality of the Act was still in doubt, and, in the words of one historian of the subject, "many of the ablest men in Congress . . . thought that Congress was going beyond its power in passing the Civil Rights Bill."[12] Indeed, several state and some federal courts held it invalid.[13]

Thus, as has often been observed, the Fourteenth Amendment was at a minimum intended to constitutionalize the Civil Rights Act.[14] Christopher Green notes that at least eleven members of Congress explicitly connected the Fourteenth Amendment with this purpose during the debates in Congress on the Amendment, and another seven did so on the campaign trail during ratification and the elections of 1866.[15] John Bingham, the principal author of the first section, insisted that the Amendment was necessary because the Civil Rights Act was unconstitutional.[16] Numerous newspapers also understood the Amendment to be necessary to constitutionalize the Civil Rights Act.[17]

Moreover, the Fourteenth Amendment had a useful purpose even for those who believed the Civil Rights Act to be constitutional as implementing legislation under the Thirteenth Amendment: the new Amendment would bake into the Constitution itself the equality requirements of the Act and therefore insulate them from change at the hands of future congresses unsympathetic to civil rights.[18] As Representative (and later president) James Garfield argued, the Civil Rights Act "will cease to be a part of the law whenever the sad moment arrives when" the Democrats come to power, and therefore it was necessary "to lift that great and good law above the reach of political strife, beyond the reach of the plots and machinations of any party, and fix it in the serene sky, in the eternal firmament of the Constitution."[19]

The Thirty-Ninth Congress was busy with other legislation as well. There was still the issue of the comity clause rights of free blacks. The Civil Rights Act took care of *intra*state discrimination against blacks, but what about *inter*state discrimination that had existed since at least the second Missouri controversy? This issue was still very much on the minds of members of Congress, for even white Unionists and Republicans were discriminated against when traveling South. Another future president of the United States, Rutherford B. Hayes, published an editorial in an Ohio newspaper in September 1865 insisting that the rebel states must "accord to citizens of loyal states who may, for business or pleasure, sojourn in Southern States the same rights which the people of those States themselves enjoy."[20]

On April 2, 1866, just days before Congress overrode President Johnson's Civil Rights Act veto, the House Judiciary Committee reported "A Bill to Declare and Protect All the Privileges and Immunities of Citizens of the United States in the Several States."[21] It provided:

> That every person, being a citizen of the United States shall, in right of such citizenship, be entitled, freely and without hindrance or molestation, to go from the State, Territory, or district of his or her residence, and to pass into and through and to sojourn, remain and take permanent abode within each of the several States, Territories, and districts of the United States, and therein to acquire, own, control, enjoy and dispose of property, real, personal and mixed; and to do and transact business, and to have full and speedy redress in the courts for all rights of person and property, as fully as such rights and privileges are held and enjoyed by the other citizens of such State, Territory, or district; ... and enjoy all other privileges and immunities which the citizens of the same State, Territory, or district would be entitled to under the like circumstances.[22]

Philip Hamburger writes that, "in light of the constitutional objections" to this bill, "Congress did not press ahead" with it.[23] The constitutional objection may have been to subsequent sections of the bill that made it a federal crime for any person to deprive others of their interstate comity rights.[24] It was not clear that the national government had authority to enforce interstate comity clause rights at all, let alone in this manner.[25]

Congress was also busy setting up reconstruction governments in the South. It enacted the Second Freedmen's Bureau Act, also over President Johnson's veto, in 1866.[26] In section 14, the Act provided that, "in every State or district where the ordinary course of judicial proceedings has been interrupted by the rebellion," all citizens of the state, "without respect to race or color, or previous condition of slavery," shall have the same rights to "make and enforce contracts, to sue, be parties, and give evidence," and so on – listing the same privileges in the Civil Rights Act.[27]

The section then added that black individuals were entitled to the benefit of all laws and proceedings for the protection of life, liberty, and property, and to "the constitutional right to bear arms." The section further provided that the president and secretary of war shall "extend military protection and have military jurisdiction over all cases and questions concerning the free enjoyment of such immunities and rights." This law in effect assumed that where the state governments failed to provide the *protection of the laws* – "where the ordinary course of judicial proceedings has been interrupted" – Congress could establish military governments.[28] When introducing an earlier version of this bill to amend the first Freedmen's Bureau Act, Senator Trumbull explained that the objective of the bill was to ensure that the federal government, "by virtue of its own authority," would step in and see that the freed people were "fully protected" in their rights if the states were to fail to supply protection.[29]

Republicans in Congress almost universally believed this Act to be a constitutional exercise of Congress's enforcement power under the Thirteenth Amendment.[30] But it was not entirely clear that the power to enact appropriate legislation to enforce the abolition of slavery could have extended to the creation of such military government institutions in peacetime – although, to be sure, neither was it entirely clear that the country had fully returned to a state of peace.[31] The Democrats thought the Act was unconstitutional,[32] and Andrew Johnson vetoed it on the grounds of several constitutional objections. "The country has entered or is returning to a state of peace and industry, and the rebellion is in fact at an end," he wrote. "The measure, therefore, seems to be as inconsistent with the actual condition of the country as it is at variance with the Constitution of the United States."[33] Johnson's veto was read and discussed in Congress as it was considering the various proposals that would eventually become the Fourteenth Amendment.[34]

Congress also enacted a series of Reconstruction Acts establishing military districts in the Southern states, although these Acts were drafted and passed after the Fourteenth Amendment had been submitted to the states for ratification. The first Act in 1867 explicitly declared in its preamble that the law was necessary because "no legal State governments or adequate protection for life or property now exists in the rebel states."[35] Section 3 of the Act made it "the duty of each officer assigned as aforesaid, to protect all persons in their rights of person and property."[36] In a series of four Supreme Court cases between 1867 and 1869, there was a serious possibility that the Supreme Court might strike down reconstruction. Each time, however, the case became moot, or the question was avoided on a technicality.[37]

The debate seems to have been over whether Congress had the power to decide whether republican governments existed in the Southern states under the Guaranty Clause of the original Constitution ("The United States shall guarantee to every State in this Union a Republican Form of Government").[38] David Currie has argued that, under *Luther v. Borden*,[39] in which the Supreme Court held that it was up to the political branches to decide what was the legitimate government of Rhode Island, the necessity of reconstruction governments should have been considered a political question.[40] Andrew Johnson in his veto message, however, deployed this very argument *against* the first Reconstruction Act:

> The United States are bound to guarantee to each State a republican form of government. Can it be pretended that this obligation is not palpably broken if we carry out a measure like this, which wipes away every vestige of republican government in ten States and puts the life, property, liberty, and honor of all the people in each of them under the domination of a single person clothed with unlimited authority?[41]

Whatever the argument may be under the republican guarantee clause, surely an amendment providing that Congress shall have the power to enforce the prohibition on the states from denying "protection of the laws" to its people would have put the Reconstruction Acts beyond any constitutional doubt? Certainly, as noted, these Acts came after the Fourteenth Amendment was submitted to the states, but in principle they were justified on the same ground as the Freedmen's Bureau bill: there was inadequate protection of the laws in the Southern states, and nationally created institutions had to step in to fill the void. The Reconstruction Act therefore informs our understanding of the objectives of the Thirty-Ninth Congress and of Congress's own views of the problems facing the South – particularly the absence of the protection of the laws.

To summarize: the Thirty-Ninth Congress enacted or sought to enact at least three pieces of legislation dismantling the Black Codes, guaranteeing interstate comity rights for free blacks and Northerners, and establishing institutions in the South on the ground that the existing governments were not adequately providing the protection of the laws. Each was constitutionally dubious. And although members of Congress were most explicit about their desire to constitutionalize the Civil Rights Act of 1866, it seems inescapable in light of the constitutional debates that Congress, in drafting the Fourteenth Amendment, sought to root each of these Acts in firm constitutional ground and further insulate their principles from future shifts in popular opinion.

THE TEXT OF THE FOURTEENTH AMENDMENT

We are now in a position to see how the Fourteenth Amendment accomplished precisely these objectives. The Amendment as ratified provides:

> All persons born or naturalized in the United States, and subject to the jurisdiction thereof, are citizens of the United States and of the State wherein they reside. No State shall make or enforce any law which shall abridge the privileges or immunities of citizens of the United States; nor shall any State deprive any person of life, liberty, or property, without due process of law; nor deny to any person within its jurisdiction the equal protection of the laws.[42]

And, to repeat, the fifth section provides: "Congress shall have the power to enforce, by appropriate legislation, the provisions of this article."[43]

What is the meaning of this glorious Amendment? "All persons born or naturalized in the United States, and subject to the jurisdiction thereof, are citizens of the United States and of the State wherein they reside." By this very first sentence, the Constitution settles the long-standing question of comity rights. By the operation of this sentence, free blacks and the newly freed people (and all others born in the United States) are declared citizens of the United States, which means they would automatically be entitled to the privileges and immunities of citizens within the several states as guaranteed by Article IV. No privileges or immunities bill would be necessary at all; the Constitution resolved this question directly.

The very next clause provides: "No State shall make or enforce any law which shall abridge the privileges or immunities of citizens of the United States." We shall explore the privileges or immunities clause in more detail momentarily because its meaning remains so hotly contested today. But its meaning seems inescapable. The Civil Rights Act of 1866 declared any person born in the United States to be a "citizen of the United States," and as "*such* citizens" they were entitled to equality in the provision of state-defined privileges and immunities. This privileges or immunities clause thus operates like many traditional privileges and immunities clauses: it is fundamentally a guarantee of equality with respect to certain state-defined privileges and immunities. If the first sentence of the Fourteenth Amendment solves the question of comity rights, the second clause constitutionalizes the Civil Rights Act of 1866 and invalidates the Black Codes.[44]

The final two clauses provide "nor shall any State deprive any person of life, liberty, or property, without due process of law; nor deny to any person within its jurisdiction the equal protection of the laws." When combined with the enforcement power in the fifth section, these provision appear to have constitutionalized the Freedmen's Bureau (and would later provide additional constitutional authority for the reconstruction governments) and to require all states to provide the due process of law and the equal protection of the laws – as understood by the antebellum legal meanings of these terms – that had been sorely lacking in the pre- and post-Civil War South.

These conclusions, if correct, are simple and elegant. The Fourteenth Amendment deploys the antebellum legal concepts of due process, protection of the laws, and privileges and immunities of citizenship, as well as birthright citizenship, to constitutionalize the legislative acts that directly sought to solve the problems of comity clause rights, private violence, and the Black Codes. Not only did the Amendment constitutionalize these various acts, but also it embedded their concepts into the fundamental law of the land itself, and it thereby insulated their requirements from change and abridgment at the hands of shifting future majorities.

By doing these things, the Fourteenth Amendment worked a radical change in our government. From thenceforth, the Constitution would impose certain fundamental equality provisions upon the state governments and allow both the courts and Congress to enforce these requirements. Whatever privileges and immunities a state accorded some of its citizens, it had to accord to all equally without arbitrary discrimination.

And no state could deny *any* citizen, or any person, two fundamental privileges and immunities: the right to legal protection for the exercise of one's rights as defined by law, and the corollary right to be deprived of such rights only on the basis of established law and fundamental procedures.

It is thus no surprise that the Fourteenth Amendment has often been described as our Second Founding.[45] From its very beginnings, our nation has been committed to the principle that all men are created equal – a commitment that the original Constitution failed to realize fully. The Fourteenth Amendment realizes that commitment. It guarantees equality not only in the rights to life, liberty, and property, but also to the privileges and immunities of citizenship, in all the states of the Union. The significance of these guarantees cannot be overstated. They completed what Abraham Lincoln described as this country's new birth of freedom.[46]

6 PRIVILEGES, IMMUNITIES, AND INCORPORATION

We have just made, over the course of this book, the affirmative argument for the original legal meanings of due process of law, equal protection of the laws, and the privileges and immunities of citizenship. We examined these antebellum legal concepts, the historical problems that had led to widespread denial of these legal protections to free blacks and others before and after the Civil War, and the public debate over the constitutional authority of the Thirty-Ninth Congress to enact various reconstruction legislation in 1866 that had sought to restore these rights. The text of the Fourteenth Amendment seems inescapably to authorize and constitutionalize Congress's legislation by deploying the specific historical legal concepts to solve the specific historical problems with which everyone at the time had been familiar.

Because the meaning of the privileges or immunities clause is somewhat more open to interpretation, however, and because it remains hotly contested to this day among originalist scholars, it is worth a more extended discussion. This is all the more true because many originalists argue that the incorporation of the Bill of Rights against the states, which used to be hotly disputed by originalists, can be achieved through the original understanding of the privileges or immunities clause. This chapter therefore changes tack and addresses four competing possible interpretations of the privileges or immunities clause and shows why they are not persuasive.

First, Philip Hamburger has argued that the clause protects only the comity rights of free blacks. Second, Kurt Lash and Akhil Amar have argued that the term privileges or immunities "of citizens of the United

States" was, by 1868, a term of art that referred to the set of national privileges and immunities listed in the Bill of Rights. Third, Akhil Amar, Michael Kent Curtis, and Randy Barnett rely on general historical background and antislavery constitutional thought to argue that there was a general public movement to incorporate the Bill of Rights against the states that prevailed among the members of Congress who drafted, and perhaps the public who adopted, the Fourteenth Amendment. Fourth, Randy Barnett and others have also argued that the clause not only prevents the states from infringing any of the rights in the Bill of Rights, but also requires that they provide a minimum set of fundamental contract and property rights. None of these arguments or readings is more persuasive than the reading advanced in this book: the privileges or immunities clause is an antidiscrimination provision with respect to civil rights defined by state law.

THE COMITY RIGHTS READING OF PRIVILEGES OR IMMUNITIES

Philip Hamburger argues that the privileges or immunities clause protects only the comity clause rights of free blacks.[1] He comes to this conclusion based on the various debates – discussed in Chapter 4 – over whether blacks were "citizens of the United States" within the meaning of the comity clause of Article IV. Hamburger claims that the privileges or immunities clause was therefore intended to settle this question and constitutionalize the Privileges and Immunities *Bill* that had been introduced in Congress, and that the equal protection clause was intended to constitutionalize the Civil Rights Act of 1866.[2]

This view is unpersuasive for two reasons. First, as explained, the original legal meaning of equal "protection of the laws" would not have covered equality in the *provision* of privileges and immunities. It would have provided only equality in the *security* of one's existing rights to life, liberty, and property. It would merely have guaranteed protection against the interference from others with the exercise of whatever liberty and property rights one had by law. Thus the equal protection of the laws clause would not have constitutionalized the Civil Rights Act of 1866.

Second, under Hamburger's reading, the privileges or immunities clause would be superfluous. After all, once the citizenship clause declares free blacks to be citizens of the United States, the entire dispute over their status is resolved: they would automatically be entitled to their comity clause rights under Article IV of the Constitution. In other words, the citizenship clause and the comity clause would together guarantee the exact same rights that Hamburger claims the privileges or immunities clause guarantees. In short, Hamburger is certainly correct that the Fourteenth Amendment guarantees comity clause rights for free blacks, but it does so through its birthright citizenship clause, not its privileges or immunities clause.

NATIONAL PRIVILEGES AND IMMUNITIES

The main alternative to the state-based antidiscrimination reading is the national privileges, or incorporation, reading of the clause. This reading maintains that, by guaranteeing the privileges or immunities "of citizens *of the United States*," the clause was intended to make national privileges and immunities – those in the federal Constitution – applicable to the states. The two principal proponents of this approach today are Kurt Lash and Akhil Amar.

Kurt Lash argues that the privileges and immunities "of citizens of the United States" had become a term of art by the time of the Fourteenth Amendment, referring only to national privileges and immunities.[3] He relies principally on the various cession treaties discussed in Chapter 3. He concludes:

> Beginning with the Louisiana Cession Act of 1803, the phrase "rights, advantages and immunities of citizens of the United States" was read as being no different than a declaration of the "immunities and privileges of citizens of the United States" and was repeatedly defined as referring to a set of national rights conferred by the Constitution itself – rights "common to all" who shared the status of US citizens.[4]

Akhil Amar similarly argues that the privileges or immunities of citizens of the United States referred to the rights in the Bill of Rights, relying on this same kind of evidence.[5] Therefore, they conclude, the privileges or immunities clause is not about state-defined rights, and it is not even about nondiscrimination; rather, it prohibits *any* infringement by the states of the privileges and immunities listed in the Bill of Rights or elsewhere in the Constitution.[6]

There are at least six reasons to believe, however, that the privileges or immunities clause is not about protecting fundamental national rights.

The Privileges of U.S. Citizenship

First, it is simply a mistake to understand the term "privileges and immunities of citizens of the United States" to refer only to the rights in the federal Constitution. Why should we? Citizens of the United States have a whole host of rights by virtue of federal statutes, too. The right to engage in the coasting trade or to trade with Native American tribes are just two of the earliest examples of privileges conferred by federal law.[7] The right to acquire patents is another.[8] When the Louisiana Purchase Treaty provided that "[t]he inhabitants of the ceded territory shall be incorporated in the Union . . . to the enjoyment of all the rights, advantages and immunities of citizens of the United States,"[9] it did not refer only to those privileges and immunities in the Bill of Rights. It referred to all privileges and immunities enjoyed by U.S. citizens from whatever source, including federal statutes.

Yet we know that the privileges and immunities of citizens of the United States derived from federal statutes cannot have been incorporated against the states. That would have given the federal government plenary legislative power. Thus the incorporation reading is unpersuasive because either we would have to interpret the privileges and immunities of U.S. citizens to exclude any rights conferred by federal statutes – which is implausible to say the least – or we would have to incorporate all federal statutes, which we know could not have been intended because that would give the national government plenary legislative power.

The key is to understand that the phrase "privileges and immunities of citizens of the United States" refers to *multiple* sets of rights. Citizens of the United States have rights defined in the U.S. Constitution, rights defined by federal statute law, and civil rights that are defined and protected by state law. The question is to which of these sets of rights the Fourteenth Amendment refers. The answer must be the third set – civil rights traditionally defined by state law – because those were the only privileges and immunities of U.S. citizens that it was within the power of the states to abridge in the first place.

This reading makes eminent sense the moment we look again at the Civil Rights Act of 1866. It declared persons born in the United States to be "citizens of the United States" and that "*such* citizens, . . . shall have the same right, in every State and Territory in the United States, to make and enforce contracts, to sue, be parties, and give evidence, to inherit, purchase, lease, sell, hold, and convey real and personal property, . . . as is enjoyed by white citizens . . . "[10] In other words, the Act declared blacks to be citizens "of the United States," and as *such* citizens – as citizens of the United States – they were entitled to equality in the provision of privileges and immunities defined by state law.

In his veto message, President Johnson explicitly tied "the privileges and immunities of citizens of the United States" to the same state-defined privileges and immunities in the Civil Rights Act of 1866. He asked: "Can it be reasonably supposed that [4 million freedmen] possess the requisite qualifications to entitle them to all the privileges and immunities of citizens of the United States?"[11] Later on in the message, Johnson pointed out that the bill "contains an enumeration of the rights to be enjoyed by those classes *so made citizens* in every State and Territory of the United States," and that these are the rights "to make and enforce contracts, to sue, be parties and give evidence, to inherit, purchase, lease, sell, hold, or convey real and personal property, and to have full and equal benefit of all laws and proceedings for the security of persons and property as is enjoyed by white citizens."[12]

Of course, Johnson's complaint was precisely that the bill purported to give the federal government jurisdiction "over the vast field of State jurisdiction covered by these enumerated rights."[13] But there was no doubt that the bill itself – the immediate context of the phrase "privileges or immunities of citizens of the United States" – defined this phrase as including traditionally state-defined privileges and immunities.

The General Public Understanding

Second, recall that the express purpose of the Fourteenth Amendment, according to at least eighteen participants in the drafting and ratification process, was to constitutionalize the Civil Rights Act of 1866.[14] These key members of Congress, and key members of the public, understood the phrase "privileges and immunities of citizens of the United States" to refer to the state-defined rights protected by the Civil Rights Bill. Lyman Trumbull, who introduced the Civil Rights Act, asked: "[W]hat rights do citizens of the United States have? To be a citizen of the United States carries with it some rights; and what are they?" He answered: "They are those inherent, fundamental rights which belong to free citizens or free men in all countries, such as the rights in *this bill*, and they belong to them in all the States of the Union. The right of American citizenship means something."[15] The author of the Civil Rights Bill believed, in other words, that the rights and privileges described in the bill were those of "citizens of the United States." And he said so just seventeen days prior to the introduction of the privileges or immunities clause.[16]

On the campaign trial in 1866, Speaker of the House Schuyler Colfax explained:

> We passed a bill on the ninth of April last year, over the President's veto, known as the Civil Rights Bill, that specifically and directly declares what the rights of a citizen of the United States are – that they may make and enforce contracts, sue and be parties, give evidence, purchase, lease, and sell property, and be subject to like punishments.[17]

In similar vein was the following poignant statement issued by a convention of blacks in Alabama in 1867:

> As there seems to be considerable difference of opinion concerning the "legal rights of the colored man," it will not be amiss to say that we claim exactly *the same rights, privileges and immunities as are enjoyed by white men* – we ask nothing more and will be content with nothing less. .... *Color can no longer be pleaded for the purpose of curtailing privileges, and every public right, privilege and immunity is enjoyable by every individual member of the public.* This is the touchstone that determines all these points. So long as a park or a street is

a public park or street the entire public has the right to use it; so long as a car or a steamboat is a public conveyance, it must carry all who come to it, and serve all alike who pay alike. The law no longer knows white nor black, but simply men, and consequently we are entitled to ride in public conveyances, hold office, sit on juries and do everything else which we have in the past been prevented from doing solely on the ground of color.[18]

Here was a forceful statement, as the Fourteenth Amendment was being debated in the states, of what the black community and the entire movement they represented was seeking: equality in privileges and immunities, whatever those happened to be. This and other public statements show that the meaning "privileges or immunities of citizens of the United States" in the context of the Fourteenth Amendment likely referred to state-defined rights. It is worth repeating that of course such citizens *also* had privileges and immunities directly by virtue of the federal Constitution and a whole host of federal statutes. But the states never had the power to abridge those rights.

Minimal Evidence of Intention to Incorporate Bill of Rights

Third, in contrast to the numerous statements in the public campaign for ratification in 1866 among members of Congress and the newspapers regarding the necessity of the Amendment to constitutionalize the Civil Rights Act, it has been widely acknowledged that no advocate on either side made explicit mention of incorporating the Bill of Rights over the course of ratification.[19] At most, one or two newspapers opined vaguely that the Amendment would allow Congress to "enforce" the Bill of Rights in the states.[20]

One important member of Congress did say something about incorporating the Bill of Rights during the debates in Congress. When introducing the Fourteenth Amendment to the Senate, Jacob Howard said the "privileges or immunities of citizens of the United States" include "the personal rights guarantied and secured by the first eight amendments of the Constitution," and that the "great object" of the Amendment is "to restrain the power of the States and compel them at all times to respect these great fundamental guarantees."[21] Howard's statement is the only statement over the course of the entire legislative history – drafting and ratification – that directly mentioned the first eight Amendments of the Constitution in the context of the privileges or immunities clause.

It is sometimes thought that, when discussing "equal protection," John Bingham, the principal author of the Fourteenth Amendment, also mentioned the Bill of Rights.[22] He asked, "Is the bill of rights to stand in our Constitution hereafter, as in the past five years within eleven States, a mere dead letter?"[23] Here, however, Bingham may not have been referring to the Bill of Rights as we understand it today. When he elaborated on the "bill of rights," he mentioned due process and comity clause rights – the exact two sets of rights that the Fourteenth Amendment explicitly adopts. Just one page before the preceding quote, Bingham said: "[G]entlemen admit the force of the provisions in the Bill of Rights, that the citizens of the United States shall be entitled to all the privileges and immunities of citizens of the United States in the several states, and that no person shall be deprived of life, liberty, or property without due process of law."[24]

By "bill of rights," Bingham seems to have been referring to the requirement of comity and due process, which were explicitly enacted through the Fourteenth Amendment's citizenship and due process clauses. In fact, this would be consistent with recent scholarship showing that the term "bill of rights" was not used as a term of art for the first eight Amendments to the U.S. Constitution until well after the Civil War.[25] Indeed, when Bingham did argue for incorporation five years later, in 1871, he used the term "first eight amendments"[26] – the same term Jacob Howard used when introducing the Fourteenth Amendment in the Senate.

The 1866 evidence for incorporation is therefore extraordinarily weak in light of all of the other countervailing evidence that the provision's likely intended legal effect was to constitutionalize the Civil Rights Act. Indeed, historian Leonard Levy has concluded that "there is no reason to believe that Bingham and Howard expressed the views of the majority of Congress."[27] Relying on Bingham and Howard demonstrates the more general risk of relying on stray statements from legislative history. This risk is particularly acute when advocates of incorporation rely on Bingham's statement from 1871, years after the Amendment was drafted and ratified.[28]

The Nondiscrimination Reading Is More Consistent with the Text

Fourth, there is an important textual difficulty with the incorporation thesis.[29] If the privileges or immunities clause was intended to incorporate the Bill of Rights against the states, then it protects only "citizens." States would be free to abridge any of the rights of the Bill of Rights when it came to noncitizens. Akhil Amar embraces this point by explaining that the Bill of Rights does quintessentially protect the rights of citizens, observing how the rights "of the people" were often synonymous with the rights "of citizens."[30] Even if that were true, it would mean that certain rights – such as those in the Fifth and Sixth Amendments, which are described as belonging to "persons" or the "accused," rather than to "the people" – would not be incorporated. Or that, if they were incorporated, they and the other incorporated rights would apply to all persons as against the federal government, but only to citizens as against the state governments. This may be good enough for incorporation work, but it is not as elegant or clear as the nondiscrimination reading.

Reconstruction Repeals of the Black Codes

Fifth, further evidence is provided by the legislation of the reconstruction governments overturning the Black Codes – the same aim shared by the Civil Rights Act that the privileges or immunities clause was intended to constitutionalize. These statutes striking down the Black Codes all spoke explicitly in terms of equality in the provision of privileges and immunities of citizenship.

Alabama's reconstruction constitution declared black Americans, among others, to be citizens and stated that such citizens "possess[] equal civil and political rights and public privileges."[31] Arkansas's provided: "[N]or shall any citizen ever be deprived of any right, privilege or immunity; nor exempted from any burden or duty, on account of race, color or previous condition."[32] Louisiana's read: "The citizens of this State . . . shall enjoy the same civil, political, and public rights and privileges, and be subject to the same pains and penalties."[33] South Carolina's: "Distinction on account of race or color, in any case whatever, shall be prohibited, and all classes of citizens shall enjoy equally all common, public, legal and political privileges."[34] Texas's reconstruction constitution provided: "The equality of all persons before the law is herein recognized, and shall ever remain inviolate; nor shall any citizen ever be deprived of any right, privilege, or immunity, nor be exempted from any burdens, or duty, on account of race, color, or previous condition."[35]

In short, when the state governments themselves, under control of the reconstruction authorities, sought to undo the Black Codes through new state constitutions, they, too, spoke in the language of privileges and immunities of citizenship.

The Civil Rights Act of 1875

Sixth and finally, a few years after the Fourteenth Amendment was adopted, Congress enacted the Civil Rights Act of 1875. This Act provided that all persons in the United States "shall be entitled to the full and equal enjoyment of the accommodations, advantages, facilities, and privileges of inns, public conveyances on land or water, theaters, and other places of public amusement; subject only to the conditions and limitations established by law, and applicable alike to citizens of every race and color, regardless of any previous condition of servitude."[36] Originally, the bill would have prohibited discrimination in public schools, too – a provision that had to be struck after Democrats won in a landslide in the 1874 elections.[37] When Congress debated the Act between 1872 and 1875, almost all of the arguments justifying it were explicitly based on the privileges or immunities clause of the Fourteenth Amendment.[38] This suggests that many in Congress only a few years after the adoption of the Amendment – a Congress that included many of the same members present in 1866 – believed that the privileges or immunities clause required equality in the provision of state-defined privileges and immunities.[39]

To recap, the national privileges and immunities reading is not as persuasive as the nondiscrimination reading. The privileges and immunities of U.S. citizens include those defined by all federal law, not only by the Constitution. The proponents of the national rights reading have not explained why we should look only to constitutional privileges and immunities. And if federal statutes also confer privileges and immunities, then incorporation cannot be correct. The privileges and immunities of citizens that are within the power of the states to abridge are those defined by state law. Those are the rights that the Civil Rights Act of 1866 declared to belong to "citizens of the United States" – a point confirmed by numerous public statements both before and after the Fourteenth Amendment's adoption. This is the reading most consistent with the text, and it is the only reading that constitutionalizes the Civil Rights Act.

BARRON CONTRARIANS AND ANTISLAVERY CONSTITUTIONALISM

Michael Kent Curtis and Akhil Amar make an additional argument in favor of incorporation. They claim that the disputes over civil liberties in the antebellum period – particularly over the free press and speech rights of abolitionists – created a movement in favor of applying the Bill of Rights against the states. This was a movement of "*Barron* contrarians,"[40] so called after the 1833 Supreme Court decision in *Barron v. Baltimore*[41] holding that the Bill of Rights applied only against the federal government. Amar and Curtis argue that there was a movement to apply the Bill of Rights to the states and that this view "would ultimately prevail in the language and logic of the Fourteenth Amendment."[42] As Curtis has written, however, most of the evidence for this proposition is to be found not in explicit references in the legislative history, but rather "in history, and ideology, and legal thought long forgotten."[43]

Randy Barnett adds to these claims, arguing that the Fourteenth Amendment reflects abolitionist constitutional thought and that, according to the abolitionists, due process of law included a substantive component, as well as that the privileges *and* immunities clause of the original Constitution protected fundamental rights generally and not only nondiscrimination.[44] These arguments, too, are not particularly persuasive.

First, beginning with the abolitionists, Barnett has catalogued the constitutional thought of more than a dozen of them.[45] Yet, as explained in Chapter 1, their understanding of due process of law seems consistent with procedural due process. Not a single statement from these abolitionists compels a substantive due process interpretation. More importantly for present purposes, their views on the comity clause were also entirely conventional: like many others, they objected to the treatment of free black citizens of the North in the South.[46] Barnett's central argument for a fundamental rights reading is that the abolitionists never inquired into how free blacks of the South were treated; according to Barnett, the abolitionists "consistently invoked the clause when objecting to the imprisonment by Southern states of Northern black sailors without inquiring into the treatment of local free blacks."[47] Yet, as explained in Chapter 4, that is the wrong comparison. Free blacks in the South were not considered citizens in the South. The comity clause entitled the free black citizens of the Northern states to the same privileges and immunities as the citizens of the Southern States, even if only whites were included in this latter category. Reviewing the writings of the abolitionists that Barnett surveys, it appears that only Joel Tiffany's writings compel a fundamental rights understanding of the comity clause.[48]

Second – turning to Amar's arguments – the number of people who believed *Barron* was wrongly decided in the antebellum period is vanishingly small. In the antebellum period, of the few judges and scholars who appear to have believed that the Bill of Rights applied to the states, most were simply unaware of the *Barron* case, and – as Amar himself recognizes – many of the discussions surrounding the applicability of the Bill of Rights to the states involved double jeopardy cases.[49] This may mean nothing more than that a prosecution for the same offense by a state and the federal government would constitute double jeopardy.[50]

The best evidence on which Amar relies for his argument about *Barron* contrarianism is a treatise published by William Rawle in 1825 and two state court opinions of Justice Joseph Lumpkin in the Georgia Supreme Court in the 1840s and 1850s, which held that the federal Second and Sixth Amendments were declaratory of natural rights and their injunctions also bound the state of Georgia.[51] But even here it should be noted that it was not the *Bill of Rights* that Lumpkin believed applied against the state government; rather, he believed that the Bill of

Rights simply described preexisting natural rights *independently* applicable against the state government.[52] Indeed, recent scholarship has shown that dozens of state-level cases agreed that the federal Bill of Rights did not technically bind the states, but was *declaratory* of fundamental constitutional, common law, or natural rights principles that independently bound the state governments.[53] And several of the cases that cited the federal Bill of Rights ultimately relied on the analogous rights in the *state* constitutions for the rule of decision.[54]

Even if some individuals believed that the Bill of Rights ought to apply against the states, that still tells us nothing about whether there was a widespread movement to enshrine this view into law. I could find no evidence of public discussion of overturning *Barron* by constitutional amendment either before 1866 or during ratification. There is also a ready explanation for why there would not have been such a movement: as described in Chapter 3, most states already protected most of the same rights in their own state constitutions. Why would there be a movement to overturn *Barron* and apply the Bill of Rights to the states when most states already protected these same rights?

It is true that, as Michael Kent Curtis particularly emphasizes, the Republican Party ideology opposed the general repression required by slavery. Hence the Party Platform in 1856 included the refrain "Free Speech, Free Press, Free Men, Free Labor, Free Territory, and Frémont."[55] This may suggest that there was a desire to make the First Amendment apply to the states. Yet this argument also does not work for the same reason: all of the states already had their own versions of the First Amendment. The disagreement between the Republicans and the proslavery Democrats was not over whether free speech ought to be protected; it was instead over whether abolitionism was "incitement" unprotected by free speech. This was a lower-order dispute about how to apply the legal rules surrounding freedom of speech to particular kinds of speech (although, of course, the abolitionists were clearly correct about this lower-order question). It was not a higher-order dispute about the necessity of protecting free speech in the first place.[56]

This brings us to the most important point. Precisely because most of the states already protected the same rights listed in the federal Bill of Rights, it would have made no sense to apply the Bill of Rights to the states. As explained in Chapter 4, the Southern governments were not repressing civil liberties *generally*; they were denying them to *blacks only*, or to abolitionists. The problem, in other words, was the *discrimination* in the provision of civil rights or, as the abolitionists explained, the refusal to extend legal *protection* to certain groups for their exercise of these known and established rights.

It would not have been necessary to incorporate the Bill of Rights to remove such unlawful discrimination. The antidiscrimination reading of the privileges or immunities clause would have already done the trick. As explained in Chapter 3, free speech and press, the right to bear arms, and all of the other state constitutional protections were privileges of citizenship in all of the states. The privileges or immunities clause would therefore now require that the states not discriminate in the provision of these privileges, and the equal protection clause would require that the states provide legal protection to these disfavored groups when exercising these rights. The antidiscrimination reading, in other words, would have solved the exact problem highlighted by Michael Kent Curtis and Akhil Amar.[57]

UNENUMERATED FUNDAMENTAL RIGHTS

We now come to the fourth approach. Randy Barnett has argued, correctly, that the "privileges and immunities of citizens of the United States" included much more than merely federally enumerated rights; they included "the rights of property and contract."[58] Barnett relies on the antebellum case of *Corfield v. Coryell*,[59] discussed in Chapter 3 and which was widely cited by the framers of the Fourteenth Amendment.[60] Recall that, in *Corfield*, Justice Bushrod Washington, interpreting the comity clause of Article IV, explained that the privileges and immunities of citizenship were "those privileges and immunities which are, in their nature, fundamental; which belong, of right, to the citizens of all free governments," including "the right to acquire and possess property of every kind, and to pursue and obtain happiness and safety," the right "to pass through, or to reside in any other state, for the purposes of trade, agriculture, professional pursuits, or otherwise," and the right "to take, hold and dispose of property, either real or personal," among many others.[61]

As explained, the privileges and immunities of citizens of the United States certainly include these civil rights defined by state law. The question, however, is *how* the privileges or immunities clause protects these rights, or what it means to "abridge" them. Barnett claims that the states could not take away these rights at all, which leads him to support the concept of economic substantive due process by way of the privileges or immunities clause.[62]

Of course, this is a possible reading of the privileges or immunities clause. But it is not the best reading. Privileges or immunities provisions in antebellum law were antidiscrimination provisions; the problem was not the general denial of fundamental rights in the states, but the denial of such rights to blacks only; and the Civil Rights Act, which the clause was intended to constitutionalize, was itself an antidiscrimination provision. All of this leads to the antidiscrimination reading. Indeed, if Barnett's reading were correct, as John Harrison has observed, then presumably a state would be able to discriminate in the provision of privileges and immunities above the floor of fundamental rights they could not eliminate for anyone.[63]

Perhaps the most convincing evidence, however, is the use of the word "abridge" twice elsewhere in the Constitution. In both cases, it seems to imply the requirement of equality. Section 2 of the Fourteenth Amendment provides that "when the right to vote . . . is denied to any of the male inhabitants of such State, being twenty-one years of age, and citizens of the United States, or in any way abridged," the state's "basis of representation therein shall be reduced in the proportion which the number of such male citizens shall bear to the whole number of male citizens twenty-one years of age in such State."[64] As John Harrison argues:

> The wording of the Fourteenth Amendment thus presupposes that one can speak meaningfully of abridging a right defined by a state's positive law, and therefore that one can tell the difference between a change in the content of the right and an

abridgment. Moreover, the historical context of Section 2 provides the classic instance of abridgment: restriction based on race, color, or previous condition of servitude. The concept of abridgment reflects the Republican notion of equality, which distinguishes between laws that set out the content of rights and laws that take rights away from a class of individuals.[65]

Indeed, members of the Thirty-Ninth Congress repeatedly stated that the Southern governments were "abridging" the rights of blacks in the Black Codes, even though they all recognized that the states themselves defined the content of such rights.[66]

The First Amendment, of course, includes the other usage of "abridge": "Congress shall make no law ... abridging the freedom of speech, or of the press."[67] This may not at first glance appear to be an equality requirement – but the freedom of speech is "abridged" in just that way when speech rights are denied to specific speakers, such as the abolitionists. Indeed, that is why modern First Amendment doctrine, with its central prohibitions on viewpoint discrimination and content-based discrimination, may be consistent with the original meaning of the First Amendment.[68]

SUMMARY AND CONCLUSION

In conclusion, none of the four competing approaches is superior to the antidiscrimination reading. The comity-only reading would render the privileges or immunities clause superfluous of the citizenship clause. The national rights reading cannot be right: The privileges and immunities of "citizens of the United States" include those defined by federal statutes, which obviously are not incorporated; the Civil Rights Act of 1866 referred to state-defined civil rights as belonging to "citizens of the United States"; and such a reading would fail to constitutionalize that Act. There is also little evidence of *Barron* contrarianism in the relevant time period, and the general suppression of civil liberty that forms the core of the evidence for this reading of the privileges or immunities clause would in fact be solved by the antidiscrimination reading. Finally, although the clause certainly refers to state-defined rights, the use of the word "abridge" suggests only a requirement of equality with respect to them. If the fundamental rights reading advanced by Barnett and others is correct, that would mean that states could discriminate above the floor of fundamental rights – and that, too, would be inconsistent with the aim of constitutionalizing the Civil Rights Act.

PART III

The Modern Era

7 THE PAST AND FUTURE
OF THE FOURTEENTH AMENDMENT

Let us briefly survey what has happened to the Fourteenth Amendment since ratification. The story is familiar. In 1873, the Supreme Court effectively wrote the privileges or immunities clause out of the Constitution in *The Slaughter-House Cases*[1] by interpreting it to refer only to national privileges and immunities. If this would have led to incorporation, then the clause might have at least accomplished something. But the Court said that it was not even within the power of the states to abridge such national privileges and immunities, which are guaranteed only against the federal government. With this twisted reading, the Court turned the clause into a tautology and rendered it useless.[2]

Shortly thereafter, probably recognizing its mistake, the Supreme Court transferred whatever antidiscrimination work the clause was supposed to accomplish to the equal protection clause. The equal protection clause was thus converted into a general equality provision, and the original understanding of that clause, too, was thereby lost. And any fundamental rights work that the clause was supposed to accomplish (this book has argued that the privileges or immunities clause was *not* supposed to accomplish any such work) was transferred to the due process clause via the concept "substantive due process." This concept, we have seen, is inconsistent with the original meaning of due process of law.

The Supreme Court did a pretty bad job of this rewriting at first. On the equality side of the equation, the Court held in *Plessy v. Ferguson*[3] that segregated schools satisfied "equality." On the fundamental rights side, once the Supreme Court decided to create a "substantive due process" doctrine, it decided against incorporating the Bill of Rights against the states,[4] and it decided instead to protect unwritten, unenumerated contract rights that it deemed fundamental. This was the doctrine that culminated in *Lochner v. New York*.[5]

Eventually, the Supreme Court reversed course on all of these: it held, in *Brown v. Board of Education*,[6] that segregated schools violated the equal protection clause. On the same day, it decided *Bolling v. Sharpe*,[7] declaring it would be "unthinkable" if the federal government were not bound by the same desegregation requirement as the states. On the fundamental rights side, *Lochner* and contract rights fell by the wayside,[8] the Court began to incorporate the Bill of Rights against the states,[9] and – more recently and most controversially – the Supreme Court replaced the unenumerated, unwritten rights doctrine of the *Lochner* era with a new unenumerated, unwritten rights doctrine by which the Court protects a whole host of social rights. For example, *Griswold v. Connecticut*[10] prohibiting bans on contraception, *Lawrence v. Texas*[11] prohibiting bans on same-sex sodomy, and *Obergefell v. Hodges*[12] prohibiting bans on same-sex marriage were all decided under substantive due process.

Thus we arrive in the modern day, with the two alternative possibilities presented in *Obergefell*: either the Fourteenth Amendment means that the Supreme Court gets to decide over time what new unwritten, unenumerated limitations ought to be imposed on the federal and all of the state governments, or it means (per Justice Scalia) that if a practice was thought constitutional in 1868, it must be constitutional today. What this book has aimed to show is that the provisions of the Fourteenth Amendment, in contrast, had well-settled meanings in antebellum law – meanings that elegantly solved the problems confronting the drafters and ratifiers of the Amendment. And while those meanings were not supposed to grant the Supreme Court open-ended discretion to make things up as it went along, neither were they supposed to constrain the Court to approve or disapprove whatever practices would have been approved or disapproved in 1868.

Let us now see how a few important cases would come out under the original meaning of the Fourteenth Amendment advanced in this book. We will start with *U.S. v. Cruikshank*[13] and *The Civil Rights Cases*[14] (the state action doctrine), and public accommodations and the Civil Rights Act of 1964. We will proceed to *Brown v. Board of Education* (school desegregation) and *Obergefell v. Hodges* (same-sex marriage), and then address the question of whether the federal government is bound by the same equality requirements as are the states. We will then jump to economic liberty and the *Lochner* and *Slaughter-House* decisions, before turning to *Reynolds v. Sims*[15] (one person, one vote), incorporation, and finally Congress's section 5 enforcement power and its interpretive authority under the Fourteenth Amendment.

THE CIVIL RIGHTS CASES, CRUIKSHANK, AND STATE ACTION

One implication of the argument that this book has presented about the original legal meaning of the Fourteenth Amendment is that *The Civil Rights Cases* (1883), and probably *U.S. v. Cruikshank* (1875), were wrongly decided.

In *The Civil Rights Cases*, Congress had prohibited, in the Civil Rights Act of 1875, private individuals from denying any person "full and equal enjoyment of the accommodations, advantages, facilities, and privileges of inns, public conveyances on land or water, theatres, and other places of public amusement; subject only to the conditions ... applicable alike to citizens of every race and color."[16] It created federal criminal sanctions against any private person who violated this law. The Supreme Court struck down the law because, it held, the Fourteenth Amendment did not prohibit any action by any private individuals, but only by the states themselves.[17]

We can now state with confidence that several of the Court's conclusions were wrong. The Court held, "Individual invasion of individual rights is not the subject-matter of the amendment."[18] To the contrary: the protection of the laws deals precisely with private invasions of private rights. Thus, if equality in public conveyances, inns and places of amusement is a privilege of citizenship, then interference with that right by other private parties comes within the equal protection of the laws clause. At least, the clause prohibits a state from denying remedies and the protection of the laws in such cases. The Court was therefore also wrong when it held that it was "not necessary to examine" the question of whether "equal accommodations and privileges in all inns, public conveyances, and places of public amusement, is one of the essential rights of the citizen which no State can abridge or interfere with."[19] On the contrary, that was the whole question: if it was such a right, private parties interfered with that right, and the state did not afford a remedy, Congress could step in.

To be fair to the Court, the central thrust of its argument was that Congress's legislation was not corrective because the Court assumed that state remedies did, in fact, exist. If discrimination of this sort "is violative of any right of the party," the Court went on to say, "his redress is to be sought under the laws of the State; or, if those laws are adverse to his rights and do no protect him, his remedy will be found in the corrective legislation which Congress has adopted."[20] That sounds right. But it was certainly fair to assume that the state laws in the South, anyway, were adverse to this right and that the Civil Rights Act of 1875 was corrective.

To put the point another way, we can think of three possible situations within a particular state. If state law were to *require* discrimination (as it did in the law at issue in *Plessy v. Ferguson*,[21] another case the Court got wrong), then that would directly violate the privileges or immunities clause. The state would be conferring more civil rights upon one group of citizens than another.

If state law were to *prohibit* discrimination, but not enforce the prohibition, then Congress could step in and supply the protection of the laws. Perhaps the Court was right to say that Congress must at least show that the states were denying this protection. Even so, the Court's language was still incorrect because such a denial of protection would not be "state action"; rather, it would be state *inaction* in the face of a private invasion of private rights.

The tougher question is the third possibility: what if there were no state law on the question at all – that is, no express requirement or prohibition of segregation? Here is where Justice Harlan's dissent kicks in. As he explained, public inns and conveyances had long been considered instruments of the state because of the public nature of the services they provide.[22] We will revisit this point momentarily in our discussion of the Civil Rights Act of 1964, but for present purposes it is enough to understand that if Justice Harlan was right, then the operators of such establishments were effectively state actors and would be enforcing at least a custom (which counts as law) of discrimination, contrary to the privileges or immunities clause. No matter which of these three situations pertained, Congress had authority under the Fourteenth Amendment to remedy it.

The same argument about state inaction might be made regarding *U.S. v. Cruikshank*. In that case, Congress had enacted a law prohibiting private conspiracies to deprive any person of constitutional rights. The indictment alleged that the conspirators sought to prevent a number of black citizens from exercising their rights peaceably to assemble and to bear arms. The Supreme Court held that the statute was inapplicable because those are rights protected against the federal government, not against the states.[23] That much was correct. But it is highly likely that those rights were protected under state constitutional provisions too, and if so, the privileges or immunities clause made equality in the provision of those constitutional rights a federal constitutional right. These black citizens were therefore entitled to the same protection of the laws as whites for their equal exercise and enjoyment of their state constitutional rights. Even if there were no relevant state constitutional provision, these citizens would still have the right to keep and bear arms simply because no law prohibited them from carrying arms. If there was no law prohibiting white citizens from carrying arms, then the same rules had to apply to black citizens. In this case, too, they would be entitled as a matter of federal constitutional law to equal legal protection for their right to carry. If the states failed to provide that protection, then the federal government could, again, step in and supply it.

PUBLIC ACCOMMODATIONS AND THE CIVIL RIGHTS ACT OF 1964

Fast-forward almost 100 years, and the Civil Rights Act of 1964 once again prohibited private parties operating public accommodations from discriminating on the basis of race, color, religion, sex, or national origin. Under modern doctrine, this prohibition cannot be sustained under the Fourteenth Amendment because of the state-action requirement imposed by the Court in the *Civil Rights Cases*. Hence the Supreme Court upheld the public accommodations prohibitions of the Civil Rights Act on the basis of the commerce clause in *Heart of Atlanta Motel v. United States*.[24]

Putting aside the question of Congress's power under the commerce clause, the requirement of private nondiscrimination in public accommodations appears quite easy to support on the basis of the original legal meaning of the Fourteenth Amendment. As Justice Harlan had argued in dissent in the *Civil Rights Cases*, the common law had long recognized that public conveyances on public highways was "a part of the function of government" and that, "no matter who is the agent, and what is the agency, the function performed is *that of the State*."[25] Likewise, at common law, "a keeper of an inn is in the exercise of a quasi public employment."[26] The same could arguably be said of places of public amusement. "In every material sense applicable to the practical enforcement of the Fourteenth Amendment," Justice Harlan wrote, "railroad corporations, keepers of inns, and managers of places of public amusement are agents of the State, because they are charged with duties to the public."[27]

Harlan's statements were well supported. Frequenting places of public accommodation – or, at a minimum, inns and common carriers – were understood to be privileges of citizenship under both state law and common law. In one particularly clear statement in 1837, for example, New Hampshire's highest court explained:

> An innkeeper holds out his house as a public place to which travellers may resort, and of course surrenders some of the rights which he would otherwise have over it. Holding it out as a place of accommodation for travellers, he cannot prohibit persons who come under that character, in a proper manner, and at suitable times, from entering, so long as he has the means of accommodation for them.[28]

In 1843, *Bouvier's Law Dictionary* explained that duties of "common carriers" include the duty "[t]o carry passengers whenever they offer themselves and are ready to pay for their transportation; they have no more right to refuse a passenger, if they have sufficient room and accommodation, than an innkeeper has [to refuse] a guest."[29] Kent's *Commentaries* similarly explained that common carriers "are bound to do what is required of them . . . if they have the requisite convenience to carry, and are offered a reasonable or customary price; and if they refuse without some just ground, they are liable to an action."[30]

It appears, then, that frequenting at least inns and common carriers, because of the public nature of the services they provided, was understood to be a privilege available to all. Thus, under the privileges or immunities clause, certainly the state – and its instruments in the operators of public accommodations – could not enforce any segregation law or custom. This appears to have been the understanding of Congress in the early 1870s – a Congress that included many of the original framers of the Fourteenth Amendment – when they enacted the Civil Rights Act of 1875, which prohibited precisely such discrimination in public accommodations.

Brown v. Board of Education

This brings us to *Brown v. Board of Education*, which had to do not with "public accommodations," but with public schools. The reasoning of the Supreme Court in *Brown* was rather shaky. The Court rejected the proposition that we should be guided by the history of the equal protection clause or its original meaning.[31] The Court instead relied on various psychological studies purporting to show that black children did worse than white children in school, suggesting that segregated schools were unequal. Not only were the studies open to serious objections, but also the Court's use of them implied that had they revealed that the black children learned just as well as the white children, then segregated schools would have been perfectly constitutional.[32]

The case for desegregation is simpler, and more elegant, under the original meaning of the privileges or immunities clause. If public education is a privilege of citizenship – and if the purpose of the segregation laws was, as everyone knew it was, the perpetual subordination of one class of citizens – then denying the same rights to this privilege is an abridgment of the privileges and immunities of citizenship. It is no different than the other rights that were denied in the Black Codes. There is nothing at all contestable or difficult about this reasoning. Public education did not have to be considered a privilege of citizenship in 1868 for this argument to work, as some scholars have argued;[33] it need only be considered such a privilege on the day *Brown* was decided.

Nor does the reasoning require reliance on questionable or contingent social science studies. If the purpose of racial segregation is invidious – and it *always* is – then segregation is inherently unequal and abridges the privileges of citizenship. Nor are we bound by whatever factual mistakes a prior generation might have believed about segregation and whether it was invidious. We are bound by the text of the Fourteenth Amendment, not by how individuals in the past expected or hoped it would apply to particular factual circumstances.[34]

There is, however, one legitimate difficulty with this argument. Recall that the privileges and immunities clause of Article IV was understood to protect equality only in civil rights and not political rights. Civil rights were understood to be positive law protections for natural rights. This would have included the rights to property and contract because laboring and acquiring property were rights we had in the state of nature; political rights, in contrast, exist only by virtue of a civil society itself. By this reasoning, it is not at all clear that public privileges – say, welfare benefits – would have been included under the protections of the comity clause. Indeed it is a little odd to insist that a transient visitor would have been entitled to the benefit of a particular state's poor laws.

Such reasoning might preclude application of the privileges or immunities clause of the Fourteenth Amendment to public schools if those are public "privileges" as opposed to civil rights. For example, Representative Wilson of Iowa argued in defense of the Civil Rights Act of 1866 that it does not mean "all citizens shall sit on juries, or that their children shall attend the same schools."[35] That is because civil rights, explained Wilson (quoting *Bouvier's Law Dictionary*), "are those which have no relation to the establishment, support, or management of government."[36]

But this argument against *Brown* is hardly foolproof. Jury service and voting and other political rights might indeed relate to the "establishment, support, or management of government," but public schools do not. (Indeed, one could argue that jury service, unlike voting, is also less about supporting the government and more about the personal rights and liberties of defendants.) Public schools and similar public privileges are arguably closer to civil rights than they are to political rights. Indeed, recall that the right to frequent common carriers and public accommodations, anyway, was understood to be a civil right. And the right to at least a private education was understood, in the case of Prudence Crandall, to be a civil right.

The question is whether public education is more like political rights or more like civil rights and public accommodations. The analogy seems almost obvious. We have freedom in the state of nature to travel, and therefore anyone who holds himself out as a common carrier must treat equally all those who wish to travel on his carrier. Similarly, we surely have a right to an education in the state of nature, free from government interference. Yet if the government holds itself out as a provider of that particular service – just as innkeepers and common carriers hold themselves out as the providers of a particular service to which we had a right prior to civil society – then the government ought to be treated just like those other common carriers. It must accord this privilege equally.

Even if one does not buy that argument, there is at least some evidence to suggest that the privileges or immunities clause was intended to reach government-provided privileges and not merely natural rights protected by positive law. To be sure, the inclusion of such government privileges is much less clear under the comity clause: it is not at all clear that a state would have had to grant a transient visitor welfare benefits. But the answer may be different for the *intra*state discrimination prohibited by the privileges or immunities clause of the Fourteenth Amendment, for at least two reasons.

First, the numerous *state* privileges and immunities clauses in the antebellum period clearly referred to government-supplied privileges as well as positive law protections for natural rights.[37] For example, recall that the Indiana constitution declared that the legislature "shall not grant to any citizen, or class of citizens, privileges or immunities which, upon the same terms, shall not equally belong to all citizens."[38] Second, the first constitutional interpreters of the Fourteenth Amendment – the members of Congress in their 1872 debates over what would become the 1875 Civil Rights Act – understood public education to be a privilege of citizenship.[39] There is, in short, at least some evidence to suggest that the privileges and immunities of citizenship included government-provided privileges as well as the positive law protections for natural rights, at least for purposes of intrastate nondiscrimination.

In sum, the result in *Brown v. Board of Education* is not preordained under the original meaning of the privileges or immunities clause, but it is certainly plausible, and indeed it seems to me to be the best answer. Public education is more like a civil right and a public accommodation than it is a "political right." And there is significant evidence that government-provided privileges were included within the privileges protected by the privileges or immunities clause of the Fourteenth Amendment.

SAME-SEX MARRIAGE (OBERGEFELL)

Obergefell v. Hodges is a difficult case under modern substantive due process – at least a rigorous version bounded by history and tradition – because there was never a deeply rooted tradition of same-sex marriage. It is an impossible case under the original meaning of due process of law, which allows legislatures to take away liberty so long as they do so by establishing general and prospective laws. It is also an impossible case under the original meaning of equal protection of the laws, which does not define liberty or property rights, but merely protects any such rights from interference by other private individuals. It is a difficult case under the incorporation reading of the privileges or immunities clause because nothing in the Bill of Rights requires that states recognize same-sex marriage. And it is arguably a difficult case under modern equal protection doctrine because it would be difficult to conclude that gay citizens constitute a "suspect class": the Supreme Court has never declared gay citizens to be a suspect class, and a key factor in being classified as such is the absence of political power.

Only the antidiscrimination reading of the privileges or immunities clause could create a plausible case for the outcome in *Obergefell*. It would go something like this. Marriage is a privilege of citizenship: no one can seriously deny that. It even comes bundled with many other privileges. Is denying this right to same-sex couples "abridging" their privileges as citizens? One could certainly answer "no," because gay individuals are still free to marry. They merely have to marry someone of the opposite sex. Once it is recognized, however, that being gay is not a choice, then gay citizens are effectively being denied the same freedom to marry that a state accords its heterosexual citizens.

In response, the state would have to argue that this discrimination is not invidious discrimination, but rather rational discrimination. After all, the privileges or immunities clause does not literally mean that all citizens have exactly the same rights. Citizens under the age of sixteen cannot drive, and they cannot drink until they are twenty-one, while convicted criminals do not get the same rights to own firearms, and so on. Recall the words of Justice Bushrod Washington in *Corfield v. Coryell*: The privileges and immunities of citizenship are "subject nevertheless to such restraints as the government may justly prescribe for the general good of the whole."[40] In other words, the privileges or immunities clause requires that one citizen be given the same rights as any other in similar conditions and that any condition must be rational and nonarbitrary.

This means that, in at least some cases, courts would have to inquire into the germaneness and rationality of the particular discrimination. In the marriage context, arguably the only rational reason to discriminate against gay and lesbian citizens is if marriage were an institution for the purpose of encouraging the bearing and rearing of children. Love is encouraged, but not required. Thus if parents fall out of love, that is no excuse for them to divorce if they have children. However, if that is no longer plausibly the purpose of marriage, or at least not the central purpose, then the argument for discriminating on the basis of an inability to have biological children becomes much less rational and germane. In a world of no-fault divorce where marriage is effectively recognized to be an institution principally about love and social welfare between two individuals, denying this same privilege to gay citizens would seem to be an entirely arbitrary and unreasonable discrimination.

To be sure, this argument is hardly foolproof. But can anyone doubt that *had* the Supreme Court decided *Obergefell* on the basis of this reasoning it would have at least appeared to everyone that the Court was genuinely engaged in the interpretation and application of existing law rather than the making up of new law altogether? At a minimum, this approach is sufficiently plausible such that it is within the range of plausible original meanings.

BOLLING V. SHARPE AND FEDERAL EQUALITY

In *Bolling v. Sharpe*, the Supreme Court held that the same "equal protection" requirement that compelled the states to desegregate schools under the Fourteenth Amendment applied to the federal government pursuant to the Fifth Amendment's due process clause. It would be "unthinkable," the Court said, were the same requirement not to apply to the federal government.[41] As explained, *Brown v. Board of Education* should have been decided under the privileges or immunities clause. Nevertheless, *Bolling* raises the question of whether the federal government is similarly bound by a requirement that it supply the equal protection of the laws, on the one hand, and also provide privileges and immunities equally, on the other. Of the three injunctions in the Fourteenth Amendment's second sentence, only one – due process of law – clearly applies to the federal government.

Starting with the protection of the laws, it seems to me that the federal government is bound by this requirement, too: it must supply the protection of the laws for those rights and privileges conferred by federal law. In the Fourteenth Amendment, there are separate due process and equal protection clauses because the Amendment is formulated in the active voice: "No *state* shall ... deprive any person of life, liberty, or property, without due process of law," and "[n]o *state* shall ... deny to any person within its jurisdiction the equal protection of the laws." A state could, of course, independently deprive someone of rights without due process by state action, and it could independently deny protection of the laws and thereby allow other private individuals to deprive other people of these rights. But a state would not itself be depriving someone of life, liberty, or property by denying the protection of the laws. It would be permitting such deprivations by others.

The Fifth Amendment's due process clause, in contrast, is written in the passive voice: "No person shall ... be deprived of life, liberty, or property, without due process of law." This provision seems to capture both the requirements of "due process of law" and "equal protection of the laws." After all, if the government intentionally denies the protection of the laws, is not the government effectively *authorizing* the deprivation of life, liberty, or property at the hands of other private persons, and thereby authorizing such deprivations in a manner other than what "due process of law" requires? If "no person shall be deprived" of their rights to life, liberty, and property without due process, then a government denial of legal protection is tantamount to an authorization of just such deprivations.

This is not to say that the Fifth Amendment required the federal government to supply protection against every kind of private violence or private interference with rights; obviously, there was no plenary congressional power to police local murders and the like (although, today, the federal government, via its section 5 enforcement power, *can* go in and supply the protection of the laws generally if a state fails to do so). The claim is only that where the federal government otherwise had jurisdiction – wherever there were valid federal laws or federal rights – the national government had to supply the "protection of the laws" so that private individuals could vindicate those rights when others interfered with them. Thus a grantee of a federal patent must have a forum (whether in federal or state court[42]) to vindicate their patent rights when those rights are infringed. And, arguably, a property owner must be able to recover property or seek damages for an unlawful search or seizure.[43]

If the federal government were to foreclose such claims even against officers exercising power in excess of lawful authority, the government would be authorizing a deprivation of liberty or property without due process by denying the protection of the laws – judicial remedies – for those unlawful deprivations. Is this not what Chief Justice Marshall had in mind when he said, in *Marbury v. Madison*, that "[t]he very essence of civil liberty certainly consists in the right of every individual to claim the protection of the laws, whenever he receives an injury," that "[t]he government of the United States has been emphatically termed a government of laws, and not of men," and that the government "will certainly cease to deserve this high appellation, if the laws furnish no remedy for the violation of a vested legal right"?[44]

Indeed, none of the framers of the Constitution would have believed that the federal government did not owe an obligation to provide the protection of the laws. We saw in Chapter 2 that the nature of the social compact required the government to provide such protection if subjects were to be compelled to obey the government. The framers would not have had to write into the Constitution any requirement of equal protection at all; it would have been understood to apply regardless, due to the very nature of free government. As it were, the framers did provide a textual basis for this requirement by providing, in the passive voice, that "no person" shall be deprived of life, liberty, or property without due process of law. The proposition that a denial of the protection of the laws would also amount to a violation of due process was accepted by many in the antebellum period, including Thomas Jefferson,[45] abolitionist thinkers,[46] and even the Supreme Court as late as 1866.[47] Due process of law, in short, required that there be protection of the laws.[48]

So much for equal protection. What about equality in the privileges and immunities of citizenship? Is the federal government bound to define and protect such rights equally? This is a harder question to answer. Some scholars have tried to show that a general equality requirement did exist against the federal government as a result of the citizenship clause (the first sentence) of the Fourteenth Amendment.[49] The citizenship clause, which has no "state action" requirement, binds the federal government just as much as it binds the states. If the notion of "citizenship" implied equality, then that notion bound the federal government.

We have seen that citizenship, at least as it was understood pursuant to the comity clause, did require equality of citizens in like circumstances. As Justice Story wrote, the comity clause "communicate[s] all the privileges and immunities, which the citizens of the same state would be entitled to under the *like circumstances*."[50] Chancellor Kent similarly wrote of the clause that if citizens "remove from one state to another, they are entitled to the privileges that persons of the *same description* are entitled to in the state to which the removal is made, and to none other."[51] This does not quite answer the question, however, which is whether the government is allowed to give different privileges based on different circumstances in the first place. The Fourteenth Amendment's privileges or immunities clause says that the states cannot give different civil rights based on arbitrary distinctions because it prohibits a state from "abridging" the civil rights of any group. The citizenship clause does not have that same prohibition.

There is some reason to think that such differences could not be arbitrary or unreasonable. Recall the words of the House committee regarding the remonstrance of the Boston memorialists on the various Seaman Acts in the South. Responding to the argument that the police power can be used to deny blacks citizenship rights, the committee argued that the police power "can never be permitted to abrogate the constitutional privileges of a whole class of citizens, upon grounds, not of any temporary, moral or physical condition, but of distinctions which originate in their birth, and which are as permanent as their being."[52] Simply put, it is not implausible to think that if "citizenship" were understood to confer certain rights – if it entails some set of privileges, whatever they happen to be – then it would follow that anyone declared a "citizen" must have the same rights as other "citizens."[53] If there is some reason other than citizenship for denying certain rights to certain classes of individuals – say, for a physical or moral condition, which might explain why children and perhaps felons are citizens, but have fewer rights – that reason must be rational and nonarbitrary.

This argument undoubtedly needs further exploration. At least two originalist scholars have argued that the fiduciary nature of the Constitution requires equal treatment with respect to all people for whose benefit government officials act.[54] Either on this basis or the basis of citizenship, perhaps some equality requirement for federal acts can be inferred. But even if there were no basis for a federal equality requirement, it would indeed be unthinkable if the federal government were to discriminate arbitrarily today; surely we can trust the people themselves to police their representatives in this regard? And, just as surely, the original meaning of the Fourteenth Amendment does not have to support every modern Supreme Court decision, however desirable, for us to understand that meaning and to implement it.

ECONOMIC LIBERTY (LOCHNER AND SLAUGHTER-HOUSE)

There has been a movement among many prominent originalists to justify the decision in *Lochner v. New York* on the basis of the original meaning of the privileges or immunities clause. In *Lochner*, the Supreme Court struck down a state law limiting the number of hours a baker could work in a week and in an individual day. The Court held that such a law violated the fundamental right to contract.[55] The only way in which a modern originalist can support this decision is by maintaining that the privileges or immunities clause not only incorporates the Bill of Rights against the states, but also protects unenumerated fundamental liberties against any state infringement whatsoever. In other words, some modern originalists have claimed that the original meaning of the privileges or immunities clause effectively gets us modern substantive due process doctrine.

As should now be clear, however, if the antidiscrimination reading of the privileges or immunities clause is the correct one, then there is no basis to strike down the New York law. To be sure, if it applied to one group of bakers but not to others, then there would indeed be a potential abridgment of the privileges or immunities of some citizens. But if all bakers are put under similar conditions, then they have equal privileges, and there is no violation of the Fourteenth Amendment.

That is not to say that extreme economic protectionism does not implicate the privileges or immunities clause. It could be that certain barriers to entry are so onerous that they ensure that one group of Americans (those already in the industry) effectively have more privileges than another group (those trying to break into the industry). Put another way, even though *Lochner* was wrongly decided, that does not mean that the *Slaughter-House Cases* were rightly decided. There, the state of Louisiana ostensibly gave a monopoly over the butchering of animals to one favored company, putting the other butchers out of business. This effectively gave one set of individuals – those favored butchers – more privileges than other similarly situated butchers enjoyed. Such discrimination would have to be justified by a rigorous analysis of the rationality of the restriction imposed on some of the butchers but not on all.

REYNOLDS V. SIMS (ONE PERSON, ONE VOTE)

A hot political topic of late has been whether the Supreme Court can strike down state legislative districts for being politically gerrymandered. In 2019, in *Rucho v. Common Cause*,[56] the Supreme Court held in a controversial 5–4 decision that such claims were not justiciable. The Justices in dissent, however, argued that political gerrymandering "implicates the Fourteenth Amendment's Equal Protection Clause."[57] That argument stems from the Supreme Court's 1964 decision in *Reynolds v. Sims*,[58] in which the Court required that state legislative districts be apportioned according to equal population.

Here is perhaps the easiest application of the argument of this book. Even if political gerrymandering claims were justiciable, they would not state a claim under the Fourteenth Amendment. The protection of the laws, after all, does not establish any rights; it guarantees legal protection only for rights one already has. The question is instead about the privileges and immunities of citizenship, which a state cannot abridge. Yet, as we have seen, the privileges and immunities of citizenship were understood to include only civil rights (and public accommodations and the like) and not political rights such as the right to vote. Indeed, if the right to vote were implicated by the Fourteenth Amendment, then the Fifteenth and Nineteenth Amendments would not have been necessary.[59] This suggests that *Reynolds* was also wrongly decided. As for racial or sex discrimination in gerrymandering, those would implicate not the Fourteenth Amendment, but those other Amendments.

INCORPORATION TODAY

Let us now consider what the world of incorporation would look like based on the antidiscrimination reading of the privileges or immunities clause. Recall that many state constitutions in 1868 guaranteed most of the same privileges and immunities that are guaranteed in the Bill of Rights; even more such rights are guaranteed today.[60] The privileges or immunities clause of the Fourteenth Amendment would require the states not to discriminate with respect to those rights. Thus we would effectively get incorporation anyway for most rights because most would already be protected by state law.

There would certainly be some rights in the federal Bill of Rights that are not protected in some of the states. Yet this outcome might be quite desirable. The states would be free to experiment with some of the more controversial rights and to push back against the Supreme Court's more controversial interpretations of them. In other words, all the basic rights would be protected, but the states would be free to disagree over whether free speech requires the outcome of *Citizens United v. Federal Election Commission*,[61] and perhaps to abolish their own versions of the Second Amendment. The states would be free to decide for themselves whether suppression of evidence is warranted for unlawful searches and whether *Miranda* warnings are constitutionally required.[62]

Even under this reading, many of the procedural rights in the Bill of Rights might be incorporated against the states by virtue of the Fourteenth Amendment's due process clause. Although most of the states had their own versions of this clause, the Fourteenth Amendment makes this a federal requirement applicable to the states. Recall the implications from *Murray's Lessee v. Hoboken Land & Improvement Co.*:[63] A violation of the federal *constitutional* procedures would be a violation of due process of law. These same procedures established in the federal Constitution might therefore now have to apply against the state governments – from grand jury requirements to confrontation. Whether all of the procedural rights protected by the federal Constitution must be incorporated against the states is a question we can leave for another day.

Those are some potential implications of the antidiscrimination approach. Although, as this book has argued, the antidiscrimination reading of the privileges or immunities clause is the best reading, as a purely textual matter the clause is, to be sure, amenable to a fundamental rights or incorporation reading. It is certainly not implausible to say that the privileges and immunities of U.S. citizens at least *include* those in the Bill of Rights and that the privileges or immunities clause is an absolute bar to infringing these rights rather than merely an antidiscrimination provision. As explained previously, under this reading the Fourteenth Amendment will not have constitutionalized the Civil Rights Act of 1866 (the equal protection clause does not do the trick), but at least it would allow for incorporation.

Is there an argument for accepting one of these other readings today? There may be such an argument, rooted in the Founders' theory of "liquidation," that is consistent with originalist interpretive methodology. As I have written elsewhere[64] and as William Baude explains in more detail,[65] James Madison understood that language was ambiguous and indeterminate; he thought that particular discussions and adjudications would "liquidate," or "fix," the meaning of otherwise indeterminate provisions.[66]

In light of the evidence amassed in this book, the best reading of the privileges or immunities clause is that it is an antidiscrimination provision with respect to privileges and immunities defined by state law. But the clause has puzzled many constitutional thinkers, and it is certainly open to contrary interpretations. And if the provision is ambiguous and one of the other readings is within the range of plausible original meanings, then they are candidates for liquidation.

CITY OF BOERNE, SHELBY COUNTY, AND THE ENFORCEMENT POWER

The original understanding that states can deny the protection of the laws through inaction has important implications for our understanding of section 5 of the Fourteenth Amendment and for two of the most important enforcement power cases ever decided by the Supreme Court, *City of Boerne v. Flores*[67] and *Shelby County v. Holder.*[68]

In *City of Boerne,* the Supreme Court held that Congress has no role in determining the scope of the rights protected by the Fourteenth Amendment. Here is the background. For many decades, the Supreme Court had interpreted the free exercise clause of the First Amendment to require religious exemptions and accommodations from generally applicable laws under a balancing test. The states had to provide exemptions for religious practices unless they could show a compelling interest why such exemptions should not be granted. In 1990, however, in *Employment Division, Department of Human Resources of Oregon v. Smith*,[69] the Supreme Court backtracked on decades of free exercise jurisprudence and held that neutral and generally applicable laws are constitutional even without exemptions – and hence, in that case, Native American tribes could be prohibited from using Peyote, a controlled substance, even though they had historically used Peyote in their religious ceremonies.

Congress disagreed with the Supreme Court's holding in *Smith* and so enacted the Religious Freedom Restoration Act (RFRA), requiring the states to provide exemptions anyway. (Recall that, under modern jurisprudence, the First Amendment applies against the states.) Congress justified RFRA on the basis of its section 5 enforcement power in the Fourteenth Amendment. If the states were violating the First Amendment as Congress understood it, then Congress could enact RFRA as remedial legislation.

In *City of Boerne*, the Supreme Court struck down the Act. Because the Court had ruled that generally applicable laws without exemptions do *not* violate the First Amendment, Congress could not enact any enforcement legislation at all because the states, according to the Supreme Court, were not in violation of the First Amendment. *City of Boerne* has been assailed by scholars who believe that the Supreme Court should not have the "supreme" or "final" say over constitutional issues, but merely a final say in those particular cases and controversies that come before it. On this understanding, the Supreme Court should have at least seriously reconsidered its prior ruling in *Smith* in light of the competing interpretation provided by a co-equal department of government.[70]

To be sure, the Supreme Court should give serious weight to a well-reasoned and competing constitutional interpretation made by Congress – but this is always true and is not unique to Fourteenth Amendment disputes. Moreover, ultimately, the Supreme Court must decide for itself questions of law in the cases or controversies that come before it. And it makes at least some sense for the Supreme Court to be the arbiter of Congress's power. If Congress could define the scope of the Bill of Rights, then not only could it define its own powers vis-à-vis the states, but also it could conclude that certain actions, including its own actions, did *not* violate the Bill of Rights.

Yet the enforcement power should not apply in the same way to each provision of the Fourteenth Amendment. Violations of due process and violations of the Bill of Rights (again, we are assuming incorporation is correct) require state action. In other words, only the government (whether federal or state) can violate these rights. It should not be up to the government to decide whether it has violated such rights or not. Thus *City of Boerne* seems rightly decided.

The requirement to supply the protection of the laws is categorically different. Such protection can be denied by *inaction*. Thus ongoing, affirmative government action is necessary to effectuate the equal protection of the laws. Government must supply sufficient courts, prosecutors, and police officers; it must supply ongoing protection for all alike. The same could be said of the Fifteenth Amendment's voting rights requirement. A state can abridge the right to vote by *inaction*, because ongoing and affirmative government action (to print ballots, establish polling places, count ballots, etc.) is necessary to effectuate that right.

The rights to protection of the laws and to voting, in other words, are quite different from those that require government action to infringe. Whether government has supplied sufficient protection or sufficient guarantees for voting rights is therefore much more a *political* question that Congress is better suited to answer than the Supreme Court. Would the Supreme Court have been better at deciding whether adequate protection of the laws existed in the Reconstruction South such that the Reconstruction Acts were no longer necessary? Did the Supreme Court have the kind of institutional knowledge that Congress routinely had from Army officers and Freedmen's Bureau officials and its own investigations? Congress, it seems to me, was clearly the superior institution to decide whether the protection of the laws had been sufficiently established in the South. This suggests that, although *City of Boerne* was ultimately rightly decided, *Shelby County v. Holder* – which invalidated the preclearance mechanism of the 1965 Voting Rights Act – was probably wrongly decided. Congress was the better institution to decide whether there was sufficient affirmative, ongoing government action to effectuate the right to vote.

CONCLUSION

There are many other implications for modern Fourteenth Amendment cases that will have to await another day. Addressing them all would fill another volume. But, suffice it to say, the original meaning of the Fourteenth Amendment is not scary. It does not mean that women, gays, and other minorities are excluded from the rights it does protect. Everyone – gay, straight, male, female, white, black, young, old, and everyone in between – gets the same protection of the laws for their lives and for their exercise of liberty and property rights. The government must accord all of these citizens the same due process rights. And it must also give them the same privileges and immunities – the same liberty and property rights – save only for those noninvidious discriminations that can be rationally justified.

This Fourteenth Amendment would be a more attractive one than the version invented by the modern Supreme Court. No longer would the Court be making things up as it went along, but neither would the Fourteenth Amendment remain stale. It would apply to new privileges and immunities, and to new understandings of liberty and property rights. Its fundamental injunction of equality would remain intact, while allowing room for the federal and state legislatures to experiment democratically with the scope of liberty and property. It would be neither too flexible nor too rigid. It would be exactly the kind of Amendment we need and exactly the kind of Amendment its framers intended it to be.

NOTES

INTRODUCTION

1. 135 S. Ct. 2584 (2015).
2. *Id.* at 2598 (emphasis added; second quotation from *Poe v. Ullman*, 367 U.S. 497, 542 (1961) (Harlan, J., dissenting)).
3. JOHN HART ELY, DEMOCRACY AND DISTRUST: A THEORY OF JUDICIAL REVIEW (1980).
4. *Id.* at 18 (noting that substantive due process is a "contradiction in terms – sort of like 'green pastel redness' ").
5. *Id.* at 28.
6. *Id.* at 32.
7. *Id.* at 14.
8. BENJAMIN N. CARDOZO, THE NATURE OF THE JUDICIAL PROCESS 17 (1921).
9. 347 U.S. 483 (1954).
10. Eric J. Segall, *Judicial Originalism as Myth*, VOX (Feb. 27, 2017), www .vox.com/the-big-idea/2017/2/27/14747562/originalism-gorsuch-scalia -brown-supreme-court.
11. *Obergefell v. Hodges*, 135 S. Ct. 2584, 2628 (2015) (Scalia, J., dissenting).
12. ILAN WURMAN, A DEBT AGAINST THE LIVING: AN INTRODUCTION TO ORIGINALISM (2017).
13. *See, e.g.*, RAOUL BERGER, GOVERNMENT BY JUDICIARY: THE TRANSFORMATION OF THE FOURTEENTH AMENDMENT (1977); HORACE EDGAR FLACK, THE ADOPTION OF THE FOURTEENTH AMENDMENT (1908); JOSEPH B. JAMES, THE FRAMING OF THE FOURTEENTH AMENDMENT (1956). Philip Hamburger collects sources on the incorporation debate that rely almost entirely on the congressional debate. *See* Philip Hamburger, *Privileges or Immunities*, 105 NW. U. L. REV. 61, 64 & nn.8–9 (2011). William Nelson wrote in 1988 that "[n]early all the scholarship dealing with the adoption of the amendment

which is addressed to lawyers is based on" the legislative history. WILLIAM E. NELSON, THE FOURTEENTH AMENDMENT: FROM POLITICAL PRINCIPLE TO JUDICIAL DOCTRINE 5 (1988) (footnote omitted); *see, e.g.*, Gregory E. Maggs, *A Critical Guide to Using the Legislative History of the Fourteenth Amendment to Determine the Amendment's Original Meaning*, 49 CONN. L. REV. 1069 (2017). *Cf.* William Winslow Crosskey, *Charles Fairman, "Legislative History," and the Constitutional Limitations on State Authority*, 22 U. CHI. L. REV. 1, 2 n.6 (1954) (noting that favorable reviews of his book referred to his "omission . . . [of] legislative history of the Fourteenth Amendment" as "perhaps the one sour note" of the book).

14.　*See, e.g.*, MICHAEL KENT CURTIS, NO STATE SHALL ABRIDGE: THE FOURTEENTH AMENDMENT AND THE BILL OF RIGHTS (1986); HOWARD JAY GRAHAM, EVERYMAN'S CONSTITUTION (1968); NELSON, *supra* note 13; JACOBUS TENBROEK, EQUAL UNDER LAW (1965); WILLIAM M. WIECEK, THE SOURCES OF ANTI-SLAVERY CONSTITUTIONALISM IN AMERICA, 1760–1848 (1977).

15.　*See* NELSON, *supra* note 13, at 6.

16.　Adam M. Samaha, *Looking over a Crowd: Do More Interpretive Sources Mean More Discretion?* 92 N.Y.U. L. REV. 554, 556 (2017) (citing sources).

17.　*Adamson v. California*, 332 U.S. 46, 74–75 (1947) (Black, J., dissenting) (relying on Senator Howard's statements in his attached appendix of the history of the Fourteenth Amendment, which, in his judgment, "demonstrate[d] that the language of the first section of the Fourteenth Amendment, taken as a whole, was thought by those responsible . . . sufficiently explicit to guarantee that thereafter no state could deprive its citizens of the privileges and protections of the Bill of Rights"); AKHIL REED AMAR, THE BILL OF RIGHTS: CREATION AND RECONSTRUCTION 185–89 (1998); Michael Kent Curtis, *Historical Linguistics, Inkblots, and Life after Death: The Privileges or Immunities of Citizens of the United States*, 78 N.C. L. REV. 1071, 1082, 1084–85 (2000); *see also* Richard L. Aynes, *Enforcing the Bill of Rights against the States: The History and the Future*, 18 J. CONTEMP. LEGAL ISSUES 77, 83–94 (2009).

18.　*From Washington: The Position of the President and Congress*, CINCINNATI COMMERCIAL, Mar. 28, 1866, at 1 (Vol. XXVI, No. 204).

19.　As William Nelson has written: "The conflicting interpretations [of the Amendment], all of them supported by impressive arrays of evidence, have left historians and lawyers wondering whether the Republicans who pushed the amendment through Congress and the state legislatures had any clearcut intentions as to what it should mean." NELSON, *supra* note 13, at 4. Other historians have described the legislative history as "not entirely consistent" or "simply ambiguous," and have said that "[c]onfusion and contradiction abound." *Id.* (alteration in original) (first quoting Earl A. Maltz, *The Concept of Equal Protection of the Laws: A Historical Inquiry*, 22 SAN DIEGO

L. Rev. 499, 540 (1985); then quoting Judith A. Baer, Equality under the Constitution: Reclaiming the Fourteenth Amendment 101–02 (1983)).

20. Raoul Berger catalogues a number of academics and Supreme Court justices who have taken this view. *See* Berger, *supra* note 13, at 99–100 & n.4, 166, 193 n.3. Some have argued that the framers of the Amendment explicitly rejected narrow language for open-ended generalities. For example, Justice William Brennan, quoting legendary scholar Alexander Bickel, wrote that the framers of the Fourteenth Amendment rejected narrow terms in favor of "far more elastic language – language that . . . is far more 'capable of growth' and 'receptive to "latitudinarian" construction.'" *Oregon v. Mitchell*, 400 U.S. 112, 263 (1970) (Brennan, J., concurring in part and dissenting in part) (quoting Alexander M. Bickel, *The Original Understanding and the Segregation Decision*, 69 Harv. L. Rev. 1, 61, 63 (1955)). Wallace Mendelson wrote that the legal phrases used in the Amendment, such as due process of law, "doubtless were designed to have the chameleon's capacity to change their color with changing moods and circumstances." Wallace Mendelson, Justices Black and Frankfurter: Conflict in the Court, at viii (1961). Historian Leonard Levy has written that these legal phrases consist in "purposely protean or undefined words." Leonard W. Levy, Against the Law: The Nixon Court and Criminal Justice 27 (1974).

21. Nelson, *supra* note 13, at 89–90, 8; *see also id.* at 61–63.

22. Eric Foner, The Second Founding: How the Civil War and Reconstruction Remade the Constitution, at xxv (2019). Foner also relies heavily on the debates in Congress. *Id.* at xxvii.

23. Charles Fairman, for example, has criticized the "unschooled jurisprudence of the abolitionists." Charles Fairman, *Reconstruction and Reunion, 1864–88, Part I, in* 6 History of the Supreme Court of the United States 1136 (Paul A. Freund ed., 1971). Robert Cover has written that the scholars who find the Fourteenth Amendment to be a product of a particular wing of abolitionist thought have "discovered roots for their own constitutional aspirations in the visions" of a minority of abolitionist figures. Robert M. Cover, Justice Accused: Antislavery and the Judicial Process 154 (1975). These "relatively unimportant antislavery thinkers" adopted meanings of old constitutional phrases "related more to theories of obligation than to the substance of the law." *Id.* at 155. Raoul Berger claimed that the abolitionists and radical Republicans in the Reconstruction Congress were generally disliked by a much larger contingent of moderate and conservative Republicans. Berger, *supra* note 13, at 234–42. My concern diverges from those of these three scholars. As I shall explain in Chapters 1 and 6, most abolitionist constitutional thought was actually quite consistent with the antebellum legal terms of art. When modern scholars claim that abolitionist constitutional thought supports substantive due process or a fundamental

rights reading of the privileges or immunities clause, it is the modern scholars who are misinterpreting the abolitionists.

24. The other is EARL M. MALTZ, THE FOURTEENTH AMENDMENT AND THE LAW OF THE CONSTITUTION (2003). Maltz also goes through the antebellum legal meanings of due process, equal protection, and privileges and immunities, and argues that the framers of the Fourteenth Amendment knew they were using legal language. Although I agree with some of Maltz's analysis, the analysis and approach of this book differs in many respects. For example, Maltz argues that due process of law prohibited class legislation and entailed a substantive component, *id.* at 4–9; this book argues otherwise. He also argues that the privileges or immunities clause was intended to be a fundamental rights provision, *id.* at 63–69; this book argues that it was always intended to be – and its legal effect was as – an antidiscrimination provision. This book also surveys more of the historical problems facing the framers of the Fourteenth Amendment and more of the legislation of the Thirty-Ninth Congress. Nevertheless, I agree with the thrust of Maltz's approach: the language of the Fourteenth Amendment referred to concepts well established in antebellum law.

More recently, Eric Foner published a book by the same primary title. *See* FONER, *supra* note 22. Foner's book spans all three Reconstruction Amendments and begins with the Civil War itself; it does not examine the specific antebellum constitutional debates or the history of the legal language deployed by the Fourteenth Amendment. And, as explained in note 22, *supra*, Foner relies heavily on the debates in Congress and also his intuition that the Fourteenth Amendment is written in the language of general principles as opposed to distinctly legal language. Perhaps unsurprisingly, I disagree with many of Foner's conclusions about the meaning of the Fourteenth Amendment.

25. When Representative Andrew Jackson Rogers asked John Bingham, the principal author of section one of the Fourteenth Amendment, what he understood by the phrase "due process of law," Bingham responded: "I reply to the gentleman, the courts have settled that long ago, and the gentleman can go and read their decisions." CONG. GLOBE, 39th Cong., 1st Sess. 1089 (1866). And when Senator Jacob Howard presented the proposed Amendment to the Senate, he observed that the senators "may gather some intimation of what probably will be the opinion of the judiciary" on the meaning of the privileges or immunities clause "by referring to a case adjudged many years ago," citing *Corfield v. Coryell*, 6 F. Cas. 546 (C.C.E. D. Pa. 1825) (No. 3,230) (discussed in Chapter 3). CONG. GLOBE, 39th Cong., 1st Sess. 2765–66 (1866). Of course, one must not place too much reliance on these legislative statements. After all, Bingham and Howard also made statements seemingly in support of the incorporation of the Bill of Rights against the states – a view that this book challenges. The point is only that the methodology of this book is just as supported by these key

congressional Republicans as is the incorporation, and several other, readings of the Amendment.

26. *See* Chapter 5.

27. *Maxwell v. Dow*, 176 U.S. 581, 602 (1900). Michael Kent Curtis also relies on this difference between legislative history and "the known condition of affairs," stating, "There are very direct statements from two leading congressional Republicans indicating that section 1 of the amendment will require the states to obey the Bill of Rights. ... Beyond that, however, much of the evidence is partially hidden in generalizations – and is to be found in history, and ideology, and legal thought long forgotten . . . ." CURTIS, *supra* note 14, at 15.

28. Is this approach inconsistent with originalism: the idea that we are bound by the original meaning of the Constitution – the meaning it would have had to the framers who wrote the Fourteenth Amendment and the public that ratified it? In practice, there is little difference between the Constitution's legal meaning and its original public understanding. As a matter of original public understanding, the ratifying public knew that the Constitution included legal terms of art and fully expected that these terms of art would be construed legally. There is significant evidence that the ratifying public in 1789 understood that the Constitution contained legal terms of art that would be construed accordingly. For example, some antifederalists had argued in the state ratifying conventions that the prohibition on *ex post facto* laws would encompass retroactive civil and criminal laws. Numerous federalists in several of the conventions explained that "ex post facto" was a term of art that referred only to retroactive criminal, not civil, laws. This was ultimately the majority view in several conventions. *See, e.g.*, Evan C. Zoldan, *The Civil Ex Post Facto Clause*, 2015 WIS. L. REV. 727, 739–40.

   The public, in other words, was aware of, and debated, the legal terms in the Constitution. Although some antifederalists were concerned that these terms of art would be construed with a public meaning – e.g. a meaning that would include retroactive civil laws under the umbrella of *ex post facto* laws – the general public understanding was that legal terms would be construed legally.

   Furthermore, it was part of *legal* methodology at the time (and still is) to interpret statutes, contracts, and other legal instruments with their objective, reasonable, and public meanings except when there were terms of art or other reasons to deviate from the objective and reasonable public meaning of a term. Blackstone wrote that "[t]he fairest and most rational method to interpret the will of the legislator, is by exploring his intentions at the time when the law was made, by *signs* the most natural and probable. And these signs are either the words, the context, the subject matter, the effects and consequence, or the spirit and reason of the law." More specifically, "[w]ords are generally to be understood in their usual and most known signification; not so much regarding the propriety of grammar, as their general and popular use." WILLIAM BLACKSTONE, COMMENTARIES 91–92 (William G. Hammond ed., 1890).

1 DUE PROCESS OF LAW

1. 198 U.S. 45 (1905).
2. JOHN HART ELY, DEMOCRACY AND DISTRUST: A THEORY OF JUDICIAL REVIEW 18 (1980).
3. The other due process clause being the Fifth Amendment's parallel clause, which applies to actions of the federal government.
4. Randy E. Barnett & Evan D. Bernick, *No Arbitrary Power: An Originalist Theory of the Due Process of Law*, 60 WM. & MARY L. REV. 1599, 1638 (2019) ("We do not think that the letter of the Fourteenth Amendment compels judges to implement the precise police-power doctrine that was developed in either the early or late nineteenth century. But implementing the Fourteenth Amendment does require a conception of the legitimate ends of government that is consistent with the original function – the spirit – of the Due Process of Law Clause in the Fourteenth Amendment; and it requires a doctrinal approach to give the text legal effect today."); *id.* at 1661 ("In the case of states," the "particular substantive limitations" are "to be found both in the texts of state constitutions and in the inherent limits on all legislative power, whether or not such limits are expressly acknowledged in a state constitution"); *id.* at 1662 ("[T]he substantive protection from arbitrary power provided by the Fourteenth Amendment's Due Process of Law Clause would be empty without an implementing construction of the appropriate ends of state power.").
5. *Id.* at 1662.
6. *Id.* at 1638, 1661–62.
7. Kurt T. Lash, *Enforcing the Rights of Due Process: The Original Relationship between the Fourteenth Amendment and the 1866 Civil Rights Act*, 106 GEO. L. J. 1389, 1459–60, 1466–67 (2018).
8. DAVID E. BERNSTEIN, REHABILITATING *LOCHNER* 9 (2011).
9. Howard Gillman argues, in his book on the subject, that a police powers jurisprudence "had been elaborated, clarified, and transformed into a workable set of doctrines by state court judges in the second quarter of the nineteenth century." HOWARD GILLMAN, THE CONSTITUTION BESIEGED: THE RISE AND DEMISE OF *LOCHNER* ERA POLICE POWERS JURISPRUDENCE 20 (1993); *see also id.* at 10 (claiming that nineteenth-century judges would "uphold legislation that (from their perspective) advanced the well-being of the community as a whole or promoted a true 'public purpose,' " while they would "strike down legislation that (from their perspective) was designed to

advance the special or partial interests of particular groups or classes.").
David Mayer argues that "[i]n protecting liberty of contract," the Supreme
Court was recognizing "the validity of the police power in its traditional
scope, as a protection of public health, safety, and morals," and basing it
jurisprudence "on well-established principles of American constitutional
law: the use of due process clauses, substantively, to protect property and
liberty in all its dimensions, by enforcing certain recognized limits on the
states' police power, limits that had become federalized with the addition of
the Fourteenth Amendment to the Constitution." David N. Mayer, *The
Myth of "Laissez-Faire Constitutionalism": Liberty of Contract during the
Lochner Era*, 36 HASTINGS CONST. L.Q. 217, 284 (2009); *see also* David
N. Mayer, *Substantive Due Process Rediscovered: The Rise and Fall of Liberty
of Contract*, 60 MERCER L. REV. 563, 571 (2009) (claiming that there was
a "long history of substantive due process protections for liberty and property rights – a body of law concerning constitutional limits on government
police powers that was well-established by the late nineteenth century," and
that the *Lochner*-era Court "was merely enforcing these traditional constitutional limits on the scope of the police power"); *id.* at 585 ("American courts
began applying the doctrine of substantive due process much earlier, not
long after adoption of the Constitution itself").

Bernard Siegan wrote that "[t]he evidence is very persuasive that
Lochner was a legitimate interpretation of original meaning," and that
"[s]ubstantive due process was a very viable concept among Justices of
the U.S. Supreme Court at the time the fourteenth amendment was
framed and ratified," pointing to a federal circuit court case in 1865 in
which the court "held that a Pennsylvania statute repealing a railroad
corporation charter violated the due course of law provision of the state
constitution." Bernard H. Siegan, *Rehabilitating* Lochner, 22 SAN DIEGO
L. REV. 453, 454, 488 (1985). Other scholars have found the seeds of the
police powers limitations on state governments in THOMAS COOLEY,
A TREATISE ON THE CONSTITUTIONAL LIMITATIONS WHICH REST UPON
THE LEGISLATIVE POWER OF THE STATES OF THE AMERICAN UNION (1868),
which is contemporaneous with the adoption of the Fourteenth
Amendment and which summarized antebellum state-level cases. *See,
e.g.*, James W. Ely, Jr., *The Oxymoron Reconsidered: Myth and Reality in
the Origins of Substantive Due Process*, 16 CONST. COMMENT. 315, 342–43
(1999); Timothy Sandefur, *Privileges, Immunities, and Substantive Due
Process*, 5 N.Y.U. J.L. & LIBERTY 115, 154 (2010) (claiming that Cooley's
"famous treatise" concluded that "the Due Process Clause protected
substantive rights against unprincipled or arbitrary legislation"); Ryan
C. Williams, *The One and Only Substantive Due Process Clause*, 120
YALE L.J. 408, 493–94 (2010). Ryan Williams has argued that although,
before 1789, there was no substantive component to due process,

antebellum courts developed a body of substantive due process law prior to the adoption of the Fourteenth Amendment. *See id.* at 512.

10. Some scholars claim that due process of law had a substantive component because it limited the legislature as well as the executive and the courts. But if this is "substantive," then it is so only in a very uninteresting sense. Of course due process limited the legislature; otherwise the legislature could abrogate the minimum process required (for example by abolishing trial by jury, or by directly depriving someone of a vested right by legislative act contrary to the existing standing laws of the land). This is also what the antebellum authorities meant when they said that legislatures could not act arbitrarily: "arbitrary" rule was rule by extemporaneous act, rather than according to standing laws. Thus scholars who have claimed that due process applies only to the executive are mistaken about the history. Nicholas Quinn Rosenkranz, *The Objects of the Constitution*, 63 STAN. L. REV. 1005, 1041–43 (2011) (arguing that the clause applies only to the executive); *Sessions v. Dimaya*, 138 S. Ct. 1204, 1242–43 (2018) (Thomas, J., dissenting) (possibly suggesting similarly). Due process did apply to the legislature – the legislature could not abrogate certain judicial procedures and could not act like a court – but it did not otherwise impose limits on the substance of legislation.

11. Although there is some historical disagreement as to whether the Latin word which Sir Edward Coke (and the American colonists) translated as "or" was understood in 1215 to mean "*and* the law of the land," *see* Nathan S. Chapman & Michael W. McConnell, *Due Process as Separation of Powers*, 121 YALE L.J. 1672, 1682 & n.17 (2012) (discussing the or/and translation), there is little riding on the question. Either formulation would require that two criteria be met for a subject to be deprived of life, liberty, or property. Whether with the "and" or the "or" formulation, any such a deprivation had to be as a result of violating known and established law, and had to be done pursuant to the processes known to the law. That is because, as explained *infra* note 12, a "lawful" judgement of peers implies some preexisting legal basis for the judgment. And "the law of the land" implies both existing law and existing procedures – although Parliament, Blackstone explained, could change both. It just had to do so prospectively. *See infra* note 37 and accompanying text.

12. Where Magna Carta elsewhere authorized certain acts, it provided that "it shall be lawful." See, e.g., clause 26 ("[I]t shall be lawful for our sheriff or bailiff to attach and enroll the chattels of the deceased . . . "), and clause 42 ("It shall be lawful in future for anyone . . . to leave our kingdom and to return, safe and secure by land and water, except for a short period in time of war, on grounds of public policy").

13. In *Murray's Lessee v. Hoboken Land & Improvement Co.*, 59 U.S. (18 How.) 272, 280 (1856), for example, the Supreme Court observed that summary

proceedings were allowed at common law when the government sought to collect embezzled government funds.

14. 25 Edw. III, Stat. 5 c. 4, STATUTES OF THE REALM 321.

15. As Chapman and McConnell explain, "[b]ecause common law remedies were inseparable from their corresponding writs, . . . it is probably a mistake to draw any sharp distinction" between the process and substance of these writs. Chapman & McConnell, *supra* note 11, at 1683 (footnote omitted).

16. 28 Edw. III, c.3, STATUTES OF THE REALM 345.

17. 42 Edw. III, c.3, STATUTES OF THE REALM 388.

18. This history is chronicled in J. R. TANNER, ENGLISH CONSTITUTIONAL CONFLICTS OF THE SEVENTEENTH CENTURY, 1603–1689, at 59 (1971).

19. *Id.* at 59–60.

20. *Id.* at 60.

21. *Id.* at 61.

22. *Id.*

23. Quoted in *id.*

24. The full text of the Petition is available at www.nationalarchives.gov.uk /pathways/citizenship/rise_parliament/transcripts/petition_right.htm. The emphasis in this paragraph is in the original.

25. *Id.* (emphasis added).

26. *Id.* (emphases added).

27. WILLIAM BLACKSTONE, 1 COMMENTARIES ON THE LAWS OF ENGLAND 125 (1765).

28. *Id.* at 129.

29. *Id.*

30. *Id.* at 130.

31. *Id.* at 130–31.

32. *Id.* at 134.

33. *Id.* at 45.

34. *Id.* at 45–46.

35. *Id.* at 46.

36. Certainly, some legal thinkers in this period argued that a law inconsistent with natural right was no law at all. *See, e.g.,* CHRISTOPHER ST. GERMAIN, DOCTOR AND STUDENT 54 (1761 [1518]) ("Nor it is not to be understood of a law made by man commanding or prohibiting any thing to be done that is against the law of reason, or the law of God. For if any law made by him, bind any person to any thing that is against the said laws, it is no law, but a corruption, and manifest error."). But this was a minority view. By Blackstone's time, parliamentary supremacy was the rule. R. H. Helmholz, *Bonham's Case, Judicial Review, and the Law of Nature,* 1 J. LEGAL ANALYSIS 325, 328 (2009). As Blackstone wrote, "[I]f by any means a misgovernment should any way fall upon it [Parliament], the subjects of this kingdom are left without all manner of remedy." BLACKSTONE, *supra* note 27, at 157.

37. *Id.* at 138 (emphasis omitted). Here, to be sure, Blackstone says that Parliament can change the proceedings by ordinary legislation – but that is because Parliament was the supreme authority in the English constitutional system, and, as Blackstone elsewhere writes, the Parliament could "change and create afresh even the constitution of the kingdom and of parliaments themselves." *Id.* at 156. The American innovation in written constitutions antecedent and superior to ordinary legislation and legislative bodies would require a slight modification to Blackstone's understanding of due process: Whatever process became enshrined in the written constitution could not be altered even by the legislatures.

38. U.S. CONST. amend. V.

39. THOMAS M. COOLEY, TREATISE ON THE CONSTITUTIONAL LIMITATIONS WHICH REST UPON THE LEGISLATIVE POWER OF THE STATES OF THE AMERICAN UNION 351 & n.2 (1868) (collecting the due process clauses from the state constitutions). As explained previously, *supra* note 11, by "due process of law" and by "the law of the land" appear to have been equivalent terms. Indeed, Sir Edward Coke, in the seventeenth century, had written that the formulations were equivalent. SIR EDWARD COKE, THE SECOND PART OF THE INSTITUTES OF THE LAWS OF ENGLAND 50 (1817 [1642]) (writing that a statute of Edward III renders "by the law of the land" as "due process of law"). And eminent judges in America agreed. *Murray's Lessee*, 59 U.S. (18 How.) at 276 ("The words, 'due process of law,' were undoubtedly intended to convey the same meaning as the words, 'by the law of the land,' in *Magna Charta*.").

40. *Bloomer v. McQuewan*, 55 U.S. (14 How.) 539, 553 (1852).

41. *Murray's Lessee*, 59 U.S. (18 How.) at 275.

42. 17 U.S. 481 (1819).

43. 17 U.S. (4 Wheat.) 518, 579 (1819) (emphases omitted).

44. *Id.* at 581–82.

45. COOLEY, *supra* note 39, at 353.

46. *Id. See* Ilan Wurman, *The Origins of Substantive Due Process*, 87 U. CHI. L. REV. 815, 823–24 (2020).

47. COOLEY, *supra* note 39, at 357–58.

48. *Bloomer*, 55 U.S. (14 How.) at 553.

49. 3 U.S. (3 Dall.) 386 (1798).

50. *Id.* at 388 (opinion of Chase, J.) (emphases omitted).

51. COOLEY, *supra* note 39, at 355 (emphasis added).

52. *See supra* notes 4–6 and accompanying text.

53. Cooley, *supra* note 39, at 355 (emphasis added) (quoting *Bank of Columbia*, 17 U.S. (4 Wheat.) at 244).

54. John Locke, *The Second Treatise of Government* § 137, *in* TWO TREATISES OF GOVERNMENT 359–60 (Peter Laslett ed., 2004).

55. *Id.* § 136, at 358.

56. BLACKSTONE, *supra* note 27, at 138 (emphasis added).
57. This is not to deny that some thinkers in the centuries between 1215 and 1787 had argued that laws against natural right or reason were not "laws" at all. *See supra* note 36. Nor is it to deny that it is possible to interpret Sir Edward Coke's decision in *Bonham's Case* as suggesting some form of judicial review, *see* 8 Co. Rep. 114a, 77 Eng. Rep. 646 (C.P. 1610); Raoul Berger, Doctor Bonham's Case: *Statutory Construction or Constitutional Theory?*, 117 U. PA. L. REV. 521 (1969), although the conventional wisdom remains that Coke was likely using natural law as a method of statutory construction. Helmholz, *supra* note 36, at 337–41 (explaining that *Bonham's Case* was consistent with the principle that "[j]udges were entitled to assume that the legislators had intended their acts to conform to the principles of the law of nature," but could not otherwise invalidate statutes). By the time of the American Founding, the principle of parliamentary supremacy was still mostly unquestioned in England. *Id.* at 328.
58. COOLEY, *supra* note 39, at 356.
59. *Id.* at 276.
60. *See id.* at 277.
61. U.S. CONST. art. III, § 2, cl. 3; *id.* amends. V–VII.
62. *Murray's Lessee*, 59 U.S. (18 How.) at 277.
63. This is a sensible approach, but it is not the only possible one. If, historically, due process meant only those processes known to the law, which Parliament could alter if it wished, then it is not clear to me why American legislatures could not alter the procedures for future cases so long as they did not abrogate whatever procedures the constitutional text expressly required. Due process of law seems to have meant only that it must be the *legislature* that changes such procedures, rather than the executive or the courts.
64. Wurman, *supra* note 47, at 826–33.
65. *Id.* at 833–36.
66. *Id.* at 837–45.
67. *Id.* at 845–47.
68. 13 N.Y. 3786 (1856).
69. *Id.* at 392–93, 395–96, 405–06 (1856). But even here the court was at least arguably trying to apply the standard vested rights doctrine. *See, e.g., id.* at 393 ("The true interpretation of these constitutional phrases is, that where rights are acquired by the citizen under the existing law, there is no power in any branch of the government to take them away; but where they are held contrary to the existing law, or are forfeited by its violation, then they may be taken from him – not by an act of the legislature, but in the due administration of the law itself, before the judicial tribunals of the state. The cause or occasion for depriving the citizen of his supposed rights must be found in

the law as it is, or, at least it cannot be *created* by a legislative act which aims at their destruction.").

70.   JAMES W. ELY, JR., THE GUARDIAN OF EVERY OTHER RIGHT: A CONSTITUTIONAL HISTORY OF PROPERTY RIGHTS 80 (3d ed. 2008).

71.   60 U.S. (19 How.) 393 (1857).

72.   *Id.* at 450 ("[A]n act of Congress which deprives a citizen of the United States of his liberty or property, merely because he came himself or brought his property into a particular Territory of the United States, and who had committed no offence against the laws, could hardly be dignified with the name of due process of law.").

73.   Wurman, *supra* note 47, at 826–36 (going through examples of typical police-powers regulations).

74.   *See, e.g.*, Chapman & McConnell, *supra* note 11, at 1712 ("The contours of this argument suggest that 'general law' interpretations of state law-of-the-land and due process clauses are not as different in basic rationale from the 'procedural' or 'vested rights' interpretations as some commentators have suggested."); *id.* at 1726 (arguing that "courts applied due process to … [legislative] acts that operated to deprive specific persons of liberty or vested property rights").

75.   COOLEY, *supra* note 39, at 584.

76.   JOHN HART ELY, DEMOCRACY AND DISTRUST: A THEORY OF JUDICIAL REVIEW 16 (1980).

77.   *See, e.g.*, Earl M. Maltz, *Fourteenth Amendment Concepts in the Antebellum Era*, 32 AM. J. LEGAL HIST. 305, 317 & n.50 (1988); Williams, *supra* note 9, at 425, 462–64; AKHIL REED AMAR, THE BILL OF RIGHTS: CREATION AND RECONSTRUCTION 282 (1998).

78.   Williams, *supra* note 9, at 462 n.247.

79.   *See Mayor of Alexandria v. Dearmon*, 34 Tenn. (2 Sneed) 103 (1854); *Budd v. State*, 22 Tenn. 483 (3 Hum.) (1842).

80.   10 Tenn. (2 Yer.) 554 (1831); *see* Maltz, *supra* note 78, at 317 n.50 (relying on this case for the proposition that due process prohibited class legislation); Williams, *supra* note 9, at 462 n.247 (same).

81.   *Wally's Heirs*, 10 Tenn. (2 Yer.) at 555–57; *see also Jones' Heirs v. Perry*, 18 Tenn. 59, 78 (1836) (describing the holding of *Wally's Heirs* as "an act authorizing the court to dismiss Indian reservation cases … was a partial law and unconstitutional").

82.   10 Tenn. (2 Yer.) 599 (1831); Williams, *supra* note 9, at 462 n.247.

83.   10 Tenn. (2 Yer.) at 608–09; *Jones' Heirs*, 18 Tenn. at 78 (describing the holding of *Cooper* as "the legislature had no power to pass a law constituting a special tribunal for the trial of a particular class of debtors to the bank, by process not known to the general law").

84.   18 Tenn. 59 (1836); Williams, *supra* note 9, at 462 n.247.

85.   18 Tenn. at 70.

86. *Id.* at 69–70.
87. 10 Tenn. (2 Yer.) 260 (1829); Williams, *supra* note 9, at 462 n.247.
88. *Id.* at 270–71 (Catron, J.).
89. 2 Greene 15 (Iowa 1849); Maltz, *supra* note 78, at 317 n.50; Williams, *supra* note 9, at 464 n.251.
90. *Reed,* 2 Greene at 27.
91. *Id.* at 28.
92. *Id.*
93. 2 Tex. 250 (1847); Maltz, *supra* note 78, at 317 n.50; Williams, *supra* note 9, at 464 n.251.
94. 2 Tex. at 252 ("[The laws of the land] are now, in their most usual acceptation, regarded as general public laws, binding all the members of the community under similar circumstances, and not partial or private laws, affecting the rights of private individuals, or classes of individuals.").
95. *Id.* at 252–53. The other cases cited by Williams, *supra* note 9, at 464 n.251, for the proposition that due process prohibited partial laws can also be explained under the traditional procedural understanding. *Ex parte Woods,* 3 Ark. 532 (1841), was about a court entering a judgment against a private person without giving that individual any process. *Id.* at 536 (noting that an attempt had been "made to enforce a judgment entered without notice or service of any process, or the privilege of making any defence to the charges against him, and upon which an execution has illegally issued, by which he may be deprived of his liberty or property"). *Sears v. Cottrell,* 5 Mich. 251 (1858), involved a statute authorizing the seizure and sale of property outside of ordinary judicial process, and the court upheld the statute at that. *Id.* at 251–54. And *Regents of University of Maryland v. Williams,* 9 G. & J. 365 (Md. 1938), involved the abolition of a corporation and the direct transfer of all its property and franchises to another. *Id.* at 409–10 ("To say that the legislature possesses the power to pass capriciously or at pleasure a valid act, taking from one his property and giving it to another, would be in this age, and in this state, a startling proposition, to which the assent of none could be yielded; and yet there is nothing to forbid it, if it is once conceded that they have the power to dissolve one corporation, and take from it its franchises and property, without its consent, and transfer them to another.").

The other cases cited by Williams as adopting a "substantive" interpretation are also consistent with traditional due process. Williams, *supra* note 9, at 463 n.248. For example, *Sadler v. Langham,* 34 Ala. 311 (1859), was about a legislative taking of private property without compensation, and the court articulated a traditional understanding of due process. *Id.* at 329 ("Another, and perhaps more valuable provision of our constitution, declares that the citizen shall not be deprived of his 'property, but by due course of law.' Without intending, at this time, to define the full meaning of the constitutional phrase, *due course of law*, it evidently does not mean a transfer of property by mere legislative edict, from one person to another."). Similarly, *In re Dorsey*, 7 Port. 293 (1838), involved a legislative act requiring attorneys (among others) to take an oath that they had never in the past participated in dueling; this, the various judges held, worked a retrospective deprivation of property. *Id.* at 367 (Goldthwaite, J.) ("Admitting an individual to be guilty, he is neither accused, tried or convicted, by any tribunal known to the laws, yet he is punished with unerring certainty and the utmost celerity."); *id.* at 368 ("These restrictions [due process] must mean, if they are not idle declamation, that no one shall be subjected to any other mode of trial for criminal offences, than was recognised by the common law."); *id.* at 380–81 (Ormond, J.) ("The term 'due course of law,' has a settled and ascertained meaning, and was intended to protect the people against privations of their lives, liberty, or property, in any other mode than through the intervention of the judicial tribunals of the country."). The other cases are all to this effect. *See* Williams, *supra* note 9, at 463 n.248.

96. JACOBUS TENBROEK, EQUAL UNDER LAW 42 (1965).

97. U.S. CONST. art. I, § 8, cl. 17; *id.* art. IV, § 3.

98. Randy E. Barnett, *Whence Comes Section One? The Abolitionist Origins of the Fourteenth Amendment*, 3 J. OF LEGAL ANALYSIS 165, 174–246 (2011).

99. THEODORE DWIGHT WELD, THE POWER OF CONGRESS OVER THE DISTRICT OF COLUMBIA 40 (1838).

100. ALVAN STEWART, *A Constitutional Argument on the Subject of Slavery*, *in* THE AMERICAN DEBATE OVER SLAVERY, 1760–1865: AN ANTHOLOGY OF SOURCES 159, 160–61 (2016 [1837]).

101. WILLIAM GOODELL, VIEWS OF AMERICAN CONSTITUTIONAL LAW IN ITS BEARING UPON AMERICAN SLAVERY 61 (1844).

102. SALMON P. CHASE, AN ARGUMENT FOR THE DEFENDANT, SUBMITTED TO THE SUPREME COURT OF THE UNITED STATES, AT THE DECEMBER TERM, 1846, IN THE CASE *WHARTON JONES V. JOHN VANZANDT* 89 (1847).

103. Republican Party Platform of 1860, resolution 8. After surveying all of the abolitionists that Barnett catalogs, I have found not a single statement inconsistent with the procedural understanding of due process of law. For an even narrower account of the Republican Party Platform that argues that the due process "plank" referred only to territories that were already free, *see* Andrew T. Hyman, *The Due Process Plank*, 43 SETON HALL L. REV. 229 (2013).

104. Perhaps it is not accurate to say slaves were deprived of liberty by legislative acts. They were deprived of liberty by private persons, and the government denied those enslaved the protection of the laws (as Chapter 2 explains). But

perhaps one could argue that denying protection of law in this sense is effectively governmental authorization of a deprivation of liberty without due process. And there is no unequivocal reason why that would not violate the Fifth Amendment's injunction that "[n]o person shall . . . be deprived of life, liberty, or property without due process of law."

105.   This argument here does not depend on the framers being wrong about how due process would have applied to slavery. They may simply have not thought about it all in 1791.

2   PROTECTION OF THE LAWS

1.   Martin Diamond, *Democracy and* The Federalist: *A Reconsideration of the Framers' Intent, in* As Far As Republican Principles Will Admit: Essays by Martin Diamond 17, 31 (William A. Schambra ed., 1992).

2.   Martin Diamond, *Ethics and Politics: The American Way, in* Schambra, *supra* note 1, at 337, 341.

3.   *Id.* at 343.

4.   Aristotle, The Politics 94 (Carnes Lord trans., 1984) (second alteration in original).

5.   *Id.* at 98.

6.   *Id.* at 99.

7.   *Id.*

8.   Thomas Hobbes, Leviathan 88 (Richard Tuck ed., 2004 [1651]).

9.   *Id.* at 117.

10.   *Id.* at 121 (emphasis added).

11.   John Locke, *The Second Treatise of Government* §§ 123–24, *in* Two Treatises of Government 350–51 (Peter Laslett ed., 2004).

12.   *Id.* § 131, at 353.

13.   *Id.* §§ 131, 124–26, at 353, 351–53.

14.   The Federalist No. 10, at 78 (James Madison) (Clinton Rossiter ed., 1961) (emphasis added).

15.   Diamond, *supra* note 2, at 344 (emphasis in original).

16.   *Id.* at 344.

17.   *Id.* at 345.

18.   *Id.*

19.   *Id.* at 355.

20.   William Blackstone, 1 Commentaries on the Laws of England 120 (1765) (first emphasis added).

21.   *Id.* at 120–21 (emphasis added).

22.   *Id.* at 121.

23.   *Id.* at 123 (emphasis added).

24. *Id.* at 129.
25. *Id.* at 129–30.
26. *Id.* at 132.
27. *Id.* at 132–33.
28. *Id.* at 136.
29. *Id.* at 137.
30. MAGNA CARTA, para. 40.
31. BLACKSTONE, *supra* note 20, at 137 (quoting SIR EDWARD COKE, 2 INSTITUTES OF THE LAWES OF ENGLAND 55–56 (1642)).
32. *Id.* at 55–56.
33. As Earl Maltz has written: "Analytically, the two concepts are mirror images. Each envisions the same core set of interests; while the right to protection focuses on the obligation of government to *preserve* those interests from outside interference, due process analysis describes the limitations on the authority of government to act positively to *deprive* people of those rights." EARL M. MALTZ, THE FOURTEENTH AMENDMENT AND THE LAW OF THE CONSTITUTION 18 (2003).
34. 5 U.S. (1 Cranch) 137, 163 (1803).
35. Philip A. Hamburger, *Equality and Diversity: The Eighteenth-Century Debate about Equal Protection and Equal Civil Rights*, 1992 SUP. CT. REV. 295.
36. MASS. CONST. of 1780, art. III.
37. *Id.* at art. XII.
38. 4 BLACKSTONE, *supra* note 20, at 319.
39. Christopher R. Green, *The Original Sense of the (Equal) Protection Clause: Pre-Enactment History*, 19 GEO. MASON U. C.R.L.J. 1, 44–72 (2008); *see also* Christopher R. Green, *The Original Sense of the (Equal) Protection Clause: Subsequent Interpretation and Application*, 19 GEO. MASON U. C.R.L.J. 219, 224–54 (2009) (showing that this was the prominent understanding of the equal protection clause post-enactment).
40. For a collection of quotations, see *id.* at 58–61. Green also quotes from Sir Edward Coke, Thomas Hobbes, and William Blackstone. "[W]hen an alien that is in amity cometh into England," wrote Coke in *Calvin's Case*, "as long as he is within England, he is within the King's protection; therefore so long as he is here, he oweth unto the King a local obedience or ligeance, for that the one (as it hath been said) draweth the other." *Id.* at 34 (quoting *Calvin's Case*, 77 Eng. Rep. 377, 383 (1608)). "The obligation of subjects to the sovereign," wrote Hobbes in *Leviathan*, "is understood to last as long, and no longer, than the power last[s] by which he is able to protect them." *Id.* (alteration in original) (quoting THOMAS HOBBES, LEVIATHAN 272 (C. B. McPherson ed., 1968 [1651])). "Allegiance is the tie, or *ligamen*," wrote Blackstone, "which binds the subject to the king, in return for that protection which the king affords to the subject." *Id.* (quoting BLACKSTONE, *supra* note 20, at 354). Seeming to invoke Blackstone, John Adams wrote in 1765: "Are not protection and allegiance reciprocal? And if we are out of the king's protection, are

we not discharged from our allegiance? Are not all the ligaments of government dissolved?" *Id.* at 34–35 (quoting John Adams, 2 The Works of John Adams 162 (1856)).

41. Minor 209, 222 (Ala. 1824).

42. 6 Mass. (5 Tyng) 78, 81 (1809).

43. John Adams, *Novanglus VII. To the Inhabitants of the Colony of the Massachusetts-Bay of the Colony of the Massachusetts-Bay*, *in* 4 The Works of John Adams 102 (Charles Francis Adams ed., 1854).

44. *Case of Fries*, 9 F. Cas. 924, 932 (C.C.D. Pa. 1800).

45. *Id.*

46. The most thorough account of this view is Melissa L. Saunders, *Equal Protection, Class Legislation, and Colorblindness*, 96 Mich. L. Rev. 245 (1997). For reliance on Jackson's message, see *id.* at 257 ("Jackson's 1832 message vetoing the recharter of the Second Bank of the United States stands as the single best expression of his party's position on partial or special legislation"); *see also* J. R. Pole, The Pursuit of Equality in American History 149 (1978) (writing that Jackson "introduced the phrase 'equal protection' ").

47. Andrew Jackson, *Message of President Jackson to the United States Senate, on Returning the Bank Bill with His Objections (July 10, 1832)*, *in* John Stillwell Jenkins, Life and Public Services of General Andrew Jackson 242 (1845).

48. *Id.* at 262 (emphasis added).

49. Jackson, *supra* note 48, at 368.

3   THE PRIVILEGES AND IMMUNITIES OF CITIZENSHIP

1. Articles of Peace and Commerce, Gr. Brit.–Port., art. XV, Jan. 29, 1642, *in* 2 A Collection of Treaties between Great Britain and Other Powers 257–58, 265 (George Chalmers ed., 1790). I am indebted to Philip Hamburger, *Privileges or Immunities*, 105 Nw. U. L. Rev. 61, 75 n.37 (2011) for this citation.

2. Declaration and Engagement concerning the Rights and Privileges of the British Merchants in the Kingdom of Sicily, made at Utrecht, the 25/8 Day of February/March 1712/1713, *in* Chalmers, *supra* note 1, at 338, 339–40.

3. John Almon, An Impartial History of the Late War 332 (1763); *see also* Hamburger, *supra* note 1, at 75 n.38.

4. 27 Henry VIII c. 26, 3 Statutes of the Realm 563. I am indebted to Christopher Green for this reference.

5. Trin. 6 Jac. 1 (1608).

6. 4 The Reports of Sir Edward Coke 5, 41 (John Henry Thomas & John Farquhar Fraser eds., 1826). I am also indebted to Christopher Green for this reference.

7. 1 ARCHIVES OF MARYLAND: PROCEEDINGS AND ACTS OF THE GENERAL ASSEMBLY OF MARYLAND, 1637–1664, at 41 (W. H. Browne ed., 1883).

8. See examples cited in *McDonald v. City of Chicago*, 561 U.S. 742, 816–18 (2010) (Thomas, J., concurring in part and concurring in the judgment).

9. Anthony B. Sanders, *"Privileges and/or Immunities" in State Constitutions before the Fourteenth Amendment* 6 & n.13 (Oct. 1, 2018), *available at* https://papers.ssrn.com/sol3/papers.cfm?abstract_id=3258765 (citing examples).

10. Articles of peace, commerce, and alliance, between the crowns of Great Britain and Spain, concluded in a treaty at Madrid, Gr. Brit.–Spain, art. XX, the 13/23 of May, 1667, *in* Chalmers, *supra* note 1, at 5, 17.

11. ARTICLES OF CONFEDERATION of 1781, art. IV, para. 1.

12. U.S. CONST. art. IV, § 2.

13. 20 N.Y. 562 (1860).

14. *Id.* at 599–600, 611.

15. *Id.* at 626 (Wright, J., concurring).

16. *Id.* at 626–27.

17. *Id.* at 608 (majority opinion).

18. *See* David R. Upham, *The Meanings of the "Privileges and Immunities of Citizens" on the Eve of the Civil War*, 91 NOTRE DAME L. REV. 1117 (2016).

19. *Id.* at 1141–48.

20. *Id.* at 1147 (noting that "the new pro-slavery interpretation sparked outrage").

21. *Id.* at 1146–47.

22. *Id.* at 1148–54.

23. For example, asserting the rights of abolitionists to speak and publish freely did not depend on an "absolute rights" reading of the comity clause. Although some in the South argued that abolitionists from out of state had the same right to speak as abolitionists in-state (namely, neither had the right to speak about abolitionism), the reality is that only Southern citizens were free to speak their minds in the South because virtually no one in the South insisted on the right to speak about abolitionism, and those who did were driven out. In other words, if one defines the privilege enjoyed by Southerners as "the freedom of speech," *that* privilege was clearly denied to the Northerners, even if the laws on the books technically forbade anyone in the South from speaking about abolitionism. None of the statements canvassed by Upham, *id.* at 1148–54, compel an absolute rights interpretation.

As for the rights of free blacks, Southerners again argued that Northern blacks enjoyed in the South the same rights that Southern blacks enjoyed – i.e., none at all. *Id.* at 1131; *see also, e.g.*, Randy E. Barnett, *Whence Comes Section One? The Abolitionist Origins of the Fourteenth Amendment*, 3 J. OF LEGAL ANALYSIS 165, 254 (2011). Yet neither did asserting the rights of free blacks require an absolute rights reading of the clause. Free blacks were not *citizens* in the South, but there were free black citizens in the North. The free black *citizens* in the Northern states, in other words, were entitled to the same privileges and immunities granted to *citizens* (i.e., white citizens) in Southern states.

David Upham argues, as does Kurt Lash, that some thinkers – including John Bingham, who would be the principal drafter of the Fourteenth Amendment – understood the comity clause to be referring to a national citizenship and read into the clause the term "of the United States" as follows: "The citizens (of the United States) in each state shall be entitled to all the privileges and immunities of citizens (of the United States) in the several states." Upham, *supra* note 18, at 1122–23; KURT T. LASH, THE FOURTEENTH AMENDMENT AND THE PRIVILEGES AND IMMUNITIES OF AMERICAN CITIZENSHIP 105 (2014). Thus, the argument goes, some key members of the Thirty-Ninth Congress believed that the comity clause protected a set of national rights, such as those in the Bill of Rights. Yet the House Judiciary Committee of the Thirty-Ninth Congress introduced a bill to enforce the comity clause rights of free blacks (and others). In a bill "to declare and protect all the privileges and immunities of citizens *of the United States* in the several states," it would have provided that every citizen of the United States shall have the right to go into any state "and therein to acquire, own, control, enjoy and dispose of property, real, personal and mixed; and to do and transact business, and to have full and speedy redress in the courts for all rights of person and property, *as fully as such rights and privileges are held and enjoyed by the other citizens of such State . . .* and enjoy all other privileges and immunities *which the citizens of the same State . . .* would be entitled to under the like circumstances." H.R. 437, 39th Cong. (as reported by H. Comm. on the Judiciary, Apr. 2, 1866, Printers No. 116) (emphases added). In other words, even the "ellipses reading" of the comity clause – i.e., a reading that included "of the United States" implicitly – was understood to be consistent with the traditional nondiscrimination reading.

I do not mean to downplay the increasing significance of an absolute rights reading of the comity clause on the eve of the Civil War, catalogued by Upham, Lash, Barnett, and others. My claim is only that the evidence for the conventional nondiscrimination reading of the clause is overwhelming and that very little of the contrary evidence actually compels an absolute rights reading. Additionally, the House Judiciary Committee of the Thirty-Ninth Congress – the Congress that would actually draft and adopt the Fourteenth Amendment – defined the privileges and immunities of the citizens "of the United States in the Several States" to be the equality in whatever privileges and immunities a particular state accorded its own citizens.

24.   LASH, *supra* note 23.

25. *Id.* at 48 (quoting Treaty of Purchase between the United States of America and the French Republic, art. III, U.S.–Fr., Apr. 30, 1803, 8 Stat. 200).

26. *Id.* at 49 (quoting Treaty of Amity, Settlement, and Limits, between the United States of America and his Catholic Majesty, U.S.–Spain, art. 7, Oct. 24, 1820–Feb. 19, 1821, 8 Stat. 252, 258).

27. *Id.* at 50 (quoting Treaty of Peace, Friendship, Limits, and Settlement with the Republic of Mexico, U.S.–Mex., art. DC, May 30, 1848, 9 Stat. 922, 930).

28. *Id.* at 51 (quoting Treaty Concerning the Cession of the Russian Possessions in North America by His Majesty the Emperor of All the Russias to the United States of America, U.S.–Russ., art. III, Mar. 30–June 20, 1867, 15 Stat. 539, 542).

29. CHRISTOPHER R. GREEN, EQUAL CITIZENSHIP, CIVIL RIGHTS, AND THE CONSTITUTION: THE ORIGINAL SENSE OF THE PRIVILEGES OR IMMUNITIES CLAUSE 29 (2015) (quoting 2 Stat. 292, 293 (Mar. 26, 1804)).

30. *Id.* at 29–30 (quoting 5 Stat. 349, 351 (Mar. 3, 1839) and 5 Stat. 645, 647 (Mar. 3, 1843)).

31. *Id.* at 30.

32. IND. CONST. of 1851, art. I, § 23.

33. ORE. CONST. of 1857, art. I, § 20.

34. IOWA CONST. of 1857, art. I, § 6.

35. 6 F. Cas. 546 (C.C.E.D. Pa. 1825). Although the case is routinely reported as C.C.E.D. Pa. 1823, the case was not decided until 1825, as the case reporter explains. 6 F. Cas. at 550 ("This case was argued, on the points of law agreed by the counsel to arise on the facts, at the October term 1824, and was taken under advisement until April term 1825, when the following opinion was delivered").

36. 60 U.S. 393 (1857).

37. As explained in note 35, the decision is often mistakenly thought to have been decided in 1823.

38. 6 F. Cas. at 551–52.

39. *Id.* at 552.

40. *Id.*

41. 60 U.S. at 583 (Curtis, J., dissenting).

42. *Id.* at 583–84.

43. JOSEPH STORY, 3 COMMENTARIES ON THE CONSTITUTION OF THE UNITED STATES § 1800, (1833).

44. *Id.* at 674–75 (emphasis added).

45. JAMES KENT, 2 COMMENTARIES ON AMERICAN LAW 61 (1827) (emphasis added).

46. *Campbell v. Morris*, 3 H. & McH. 535, 553–54 (Md. 1797).

47. *Lavery v. Woodland*, 2 Del. Cas. 299, 307 (1817).

48. *Id.* at 307–08.

49. *Abbott v. Bayley*, 23 Mass. (6 Pick.) 89, 92 (1827).
50. *Id.* at 92–93.
51. 11 Stat. 611, 612 (1855).
52. 8 Op. Att'y Gen. 300, 302 (1857).
53. Lash, *supra* note 23, at 25–26 (footnote omitted).
54. *See, e.g.*, Cong. Globe, 39th Cong., 1st Sess. 599 (Trumbull) ("This bill [the Civil Rights Act of 1866] is applicable exclusively to civil rights. It does not propose to regulate the political rights of individuals: it has nothing to do with the right of suffrage or any other political right; but is simply intended to carry out a constitutional provision, and guaranty to every person of every color the same civil rights."); *id.* at 1117 (Wilson) (noting that civil rights do not include the "political right" of suffrage or jury service); *id.* at 2542 (Bingham) ("The [draft Fourteenth] amendment does not give, as the second section shows, the power to Congress of regulating suffrage in the several states."); *id.* at 2766 (Howard) (noting that the first section of the Fourteenth Amendment, which includes the privileges or immunities clause, "does not give to either of these classes the right of voting").
55. Thomas M. Cooley, Treatise on the Constitutional Limitations which Rest upon the Legislative Power of the States of the American Union (1868).
56. *Id.* at 303 (footnote omitted).
57. *Id.* at 303–08.
58. *Id.* at 308.
59. *Id.* at 309.
60. *Id.* at 310–11.
61. *Id.* at 311.
62. *Id.* at 312, 318.
63. *Id.* at 325–26.
64. *Id.* at 328.
65. *Id.* at 334.
66. *Id.* at 347.
67. *Id.* at 349 (quoting Story, *supra* note 43, at § 1894).
68. *Id.* at 350.
69. *Id.* at 351 & n.2.
70. *Id.* at 414.
71. *Id.* at 467.
72. *Id.* at 469–70 (emphasis added).
73. Cooley does not enumerate the number of states, but presumes the requirement that takings must be for public use and justly compensated as a constitutional principle. *Id.* at 523–62. Steven G. Calabresi and Sarah E. Agudo have shown that thirty-three states in 1868 had a takings clause. Steven G. Calabresi & Sarah E. Agudo, *Individual Rights under State Constitutions When the Fourteenth Amendment Was Ratified in 1868: What*

Rights Are Deeply Rooted in American History and Tradition?, 87 Tex. L. Rev. 7, 72 (2008).

74. *Id.* at 23.

4   ABRIDGMENT OF RIGHTS BEFORE AND AFTER THE CIVIL WAR

1. 60 U.S. (19 How.) 393 (1857).
2. 20 N.Y. 562 (1860).
3. 6 F. Cas. 546 (C.C.E.D. Pa. 1825).
4. William M. Wiecek, The Sources of Anti-Slavery Constitutionalism in America, 1760–1848, at 122–23 (1977) (quoting Mo. Const. of 1820, art. III, § 26, *in* 4 Federal and State Constitutions 2154 (Francis Newton Thorpe ed., 1909)).
5. 37 Annals of Cong. 108 (Joseph Gales & William W. Seaton eds., 1855) (emphasis added).
6. *Id.* at 513–14.
7. *Id.* at 529–31.
8. *Id.* at 536.
9. *Id.* at 537.
10. *Id.* at 538.
11. *Id.* at 538–39.
12. *Id.* at 539.
13. *Id.* at 544.
14. *Id.* at 545–46.
15. *Id.* at 550.
16. *Id.* at 553.
17. *Id.* at 555.
18. *Id.* at 556.
19. *Id.* at 557.
20. *Id.* at 571.
21. *Id.* at 596.
22. *Id.*
23. *Id.* at 636.
24. *Id.* at 1134; *see also* Wiecek, *supra* note 4, at 123.
25. 37 Annals of Cong. 1110 (1821).
26. *Id.* at 1228; *see also* Wiecek, *supra* note 4, at 124.
27. And, as Martha Jones recently reminded us, so did Maryland. Martha S. Jones, Birthright Citizens: A History of Race and Rights in Antebellum America 25, 31–33 (2018).
28. Ind. Const. of 1851, art. XIII, § 1.

29.   Proceedings of the Ohio Anti-Slavery Convention, held at Putnam, on the Twenty-Second, Twenty-Third, and Twenty-Fourth of April, 1835, at 36–40.

30.   *Id.* at 36–39.

31.   *Id.* at 38.

32.   *Id.*

33.   Cong. Globe, 35th Cong., 2d Sess. 984 (1859).

34.   *Id.*

35.   *Id.* at 985.

36.   WIECEK, *supra* note 4, at 129.

37.   *Id.* at 132.

38.   *Id.* (citing ACTS AND RESOLUTIONS OF THE GENERAL ASSEMBLY OF THE STATE OF SOUTH CAROLINA 11–14 (Daniel Faust ed., 1823)).

39.   *Id.* at 137 (citing Comm. on Commerce, 27th Cong., Rep. on Free Colored Seamen – Majority and Minority Reps. 35 (Comm. Print. 1843)).

40.   *Id.* at 138.

41.   *Id.* at 139.

42.   MR. JUSTICE 210, 213 (Allison Dunham & Philip B. Kurland eds., 1956); *see also* WIECEK, *supra* note 4, at 139.

43.   Rep. on Free Colored Seamen, *supra* note 39, at 2.

44.   *Id.* at 3–4.

45.   *Id.* at 37–49; *see also* WIECEK, *supra* note 4, at 139–40.

46.   WIECEK, *supra* note 4, at 140.

47.   South Carolina Resolution on the Mission of Samuel Hoar, Dec. 5, 1844, *in* STATE DOCUMENTS ON FEDERAL RELATIONS 237–38 (Herman V. Ames ed., 1906).

48.   Proceedings of the United States Senate on the Fugitive Slave Bill, – The Abolition of the Slave-Trade in the District of Columbia, – and the Imprisonment of Free Colored Seamen in the Southern Ports 36 (1850).

49.   WIECEK, *supra* note 4, at 163.

50.   *Id.*

51.   *Crandall v. State*, 10 Conn. 339, 342 (Conn. 1834).

52.   *Id.* at 343–44.

53.   *Id.* at 344.

54.   *Id.* at 347 (emphases omitted).

55.   *Id.* at 357.

56.   *Id.* at 367–72.

57.   WIECEK, *supra* note 4, at 164; *Opinion of the Judges of the Supreme Court*, 32 Conn. 565 (Conn. 1865).

58.   WIECEK, *supra* note 4, at 164.

59.   *Dred Scott*, 60 U.S. (19 How.) at 431–32; ELBERT WILLIAM R. EWING, LEGAL AND HISTORICAL STATUS OF THE *DRED SCOTT* DECISION 25–27 (1908);

MICHAEL STOKES PAULSEN ET AL., THE CONSTITUTION OF THE UNITED STATES 733–34 (3d ed. 2017).

60. *Dred Scott*, 60 U.S. (19 How.) at 403.

61. *Id.* at 404–05.

62. *Id.* at 405–07.

63. *Id.* at 572–73, 576–78 (Curtis, J., dissenting).

64. Abraham Lincoln, *The "Divided House" Speech Delivered at Springfield, Illinois, on His Nomination to the Senate of the United States (June 17, 1858)*, *in* ABRAHAM LINCOLN'S SPEECHES 71, 77 (L. E. Chittenden ed., 1908).

65. Stephen Douglas, *Speech of Senator Douglas on the Occasion of His Public Reception at Chicago (July 9, 1858)*, *in* POLITICAL DEBATES BETWEEN ABRAHAM LINCOLN AND STEPHEN A. DOUGLAS 8, 17 (1895) (paragraph break added).

66. WIECEK, *supra* note 4, at 172–73.

67. *Id.* at 173.

68. *Id.*

69. *Id.* at 174 (quoting Letter from Amos Kendall to Alfred Huger, Aug. 4, 1835).

70. *Id.* at 175.

71. *Id.* at 175–77.

72. *Id.* at 177.

73. *Id.* at 179 (quoting An Act to Prevent the Publication or Circulation in this State of Seditious Pamphlets and Papers, *in* Public Acts Passed at the First Session of the Twenty-First General Assembly of the State of Tennessee, 1835–6, at 145–46 (1836)).

74. *Id.* at 179–80.

75. *Id.* at 180.

76. *Id.* at 181–82 (quoting Resolution of Nov. 16, 1836, *in* Acts Passed by the Legislature of the State of Vermont, at their October Session, 1836, at 44 (1836)).

77. *Id.* at 178.

78. *Id.* at 182–83 (quoting Proceedings of the New York Anti-Slavery Convention, Held at Utica, October 21, and New York Anti-Slavery Society, Held at Peterboro', October 22, 1835, at 16 (1835)).

79. *Id.* at 183 (quoting *Letter from James G. Birney to Gerrit Smith, 13 Sept. 1835*, *in* LETTERS OF JAMES GILLESPIE BIRNEY, 1831–1857, at 343 (Dwight L. Dumond ed., 1938)).

80. Akhil Reed Amar, *The Bill of Rights and the Fourteenth Amendment*, 101 YALE L.J. 1193, 1216 (1992).

81. MICHAEL KENT CURTIS, NO STATE SHALL ABRIDGE: THE FOURTEENTH AMENDMENT AND THE BILL OF RIGHTS 31–32 (1986). A more recent book makes the intriguing argument that slavery was the critical manifestation of Southern oligarchy, and the general suppression of civil liberties was

necessary not only to maintain slavery, but also to maintain this oligarchic power. Forrest A. Nabors, From Oligarchy to Republicanism: The Great Task of Reconstruction 73–77 (2017).

82. Curtis, *supra* note 81, at 31.

83. Jacobus tenBroek, Equal under Law 36 (1965).

84. *Id.*

85. Michael Kent Curtis, The 1837 Killing of Elijah Lovejoy by an Anti-Abolition Mob: Free Speech, Mobs, Republican Government, and the Privileges of American Citizens, 44 UCLA L. Rev. 1109, 1110 (1997).

86. *Id.* at 1124–26. For a thorough account of other mob violence against abolitionist presses, see Fourth Annual Report of the American Anti-Slavery Society 78–89 (1837).

87. tenBroek, *supra* note 83, at 37.

88. *Id.* at 37–38 (emphasis added).

89. *Id.* at 38 n. 6 (quoting Joseph C. Lovejoy & Owen Lovejoy, Memoir of the Rev. Elijah Lovejoy; Who Was Murdered in Defence of the Liberty of the Press, at Alton, Illinois, Nov. 7, 1837, at 279–80 (1838)).

90. *Id.* (quoting William Goodell, Emancipator, July 22, 1834).

91. Abraham Lincoln, Abraham Lincoln: His Speeches and Writings 77 (Roy P. Basler ed., 1946).

92. *Id.* at 77–78

93. Harry V. Jaffa, Crisis of the House Divided: An Interpretation of the Issues in the Lincoln–Douglas Debates 196–99 (50th anniv. ed. 2009 [1959]).

94. Lincoln, *supra* note 91, at 78.

95. *Id.*

96. *Id.*

97. *Id.* at 79.

98. *Id.* at 80.

99. *Id.* at 80.

100. M. L. Bennett, The Vermont Justice, Being a Treatise on the Civil and Criminal Jurisdiction of Justices of the Peace 567–68 (1864). I am indebted to Christopher R. Green, *The Original Sense of the (Equal) Protection Clause: Pre-enacting History*, 19 Geo. Mason U. C.R. L.J. 1, 49–51 (2008), for this and the following related citations.

101. Francis Wharton, 3 A Treatise on the Criminal Law of the United States § 2768, at 310 (6th ed. 1868).

102. William Conyngham Plunket, *Speech on the "Peterloo Massacre," in* 1 The Life, Letters, and Speeches of Lord Plunket 373, 386–87 (David Plunket ed., 1867).

103. *Id.*

104. Eric Foner, The Second Founding: How the Civil War and Reconstruction Remade the Constitution 79 (2019). For the actual

article, see Equal Protection under the Law, National Anti-Slavery Standard, Aug. 29, 1863, *available at* https://archive.org/details/3d87de5d-1f55-4187-b4fc-565c420214cd.

105. This argument was advanced most lucidly by Theodore Weld in a pamphlet on the power of Congress over slavery in the District of Columbia, which Jacobus tenBroek describes as one "of the more important tracts of the antislavery movement" that helped to "define a pattern of argument followed by many lesser speakers and pamphleteers." TENBROEK, *supra* note 83, at 49. To emancipate the slaves, wrote Weld, is "to prevent by legal restraints one class of men from seizing upon another class, and robbing them at pleasure of their earnings, their time, their liberty, their kindred, and the very use and ownership of their own persons." He then connected this argument to the protection of law: "It has been already shown that allegiance is exacted of the slave. Is the government of the United States unable to grant protection where it exacts allegiance?" *Id.* at 48 (quoting THEODORE DWIGHT WELD, THE POWER OF CONGRESS OVER SLAVERY IN THE DISTRICT OF COLUMBIA (1838)). *See generally* Randy E. Barnett, *Whence Comes Section One? The Abolitionist Origins of the Fourteenth Amendment*, 3 J. OF LEGAL ANALYSIS 165 (2011) (cataloguing similar abolitionist statements about slavery and the protection of the laws).

Second, the federal government denied free blacks the protection of the laws and authorized deprivations of their liberty without due process by enactment of the fugitive slave laws. The Fugitive Slave Act of 1793 accorded runaway slaves (and alleged slaves) the barest of legal process. The Fugitive Slave Act of 1850, enacted as part of the Compromise of 1850, was even worse: The capture of the allegedly runaway slaves could be done with no process at all; the alleged runaway was expressly forbidden from testifying; the writ of habeas corpus was forbidden; and the fee paid to the commissioners who decided on the validity of the capture was twice as much if the commissioner found in favor of the owner. These requirements made it easy for kidnappers to seize free blacks in the border states. HAROLD M. HYMAN & WILLIAM M. WIECEK, EQUAL JUSTICE UNDER LAW 149–50 (1982).

106. *Monthly Record of Current Events*, 32 HARPER'S NEW MONTHLY MAGAZINE 805, 807–08 (1866).

107. WILLIAM E. NELSON, THE FOURTEENTH AMENDMENT: FROM POLITICAL PRINCIPLE TO JUDICIAL DOCTRINE 42 (1988) (quoting Letter of Lyman Trumbull to Mrs. Gary, June 27, 1866).

108. *Monthly Record of Current Events*, 33 HARPER'S NEW MONTHLY MAGAZINE 669, 671 (1866). For the references in this paragraph, I am indebted to NELSON, *supra* note 107, at 42.

109. HYMAN & WIECEK, *supra* note 105, at 324.

110. Paul Finkleman, *The Historical Context of the 14th Amendment, in* INFINITE HOPE AND FINITE DISAPPOINTMENT: THE STORY OF THE FIRST INTERPRETERS OF THE FOURTEENTH AMENDMENT 36, 47–50 (Elizabeth Reilly ed., 2011).

111. *Id.* at 50.

112. Reported in Cong. Globe, 39th Cong., 1st Sess. 1834 (1866).

113. Ulysses S. Grant, General Orders No. 44 (1866), *reprinted in* 16 THE PAPERS OF ULYSSES S. GRANT 228, 228 (John Y. Simon ed., 1988). Instances of outrages against military officers and freedmen are catalogued in *id.* at 228–30.

114. Letter from Ulysses S. Grant to George H. Thomas (July 6, 1866), *in id.* at 230. One Freedmen's Bureau officer reported to Senator Sumner in 1866 that judges and peace officers were ignoring complaints from blacks, but acted with "eagerness and severity" when whites complained against blacks and that terror and extortion were keeping blacks down. HYMAN & WIECEK, *supra* note 105, at 423–24 (citing Letter of S.C. Gardner to Charles Sumner, Nov. 19, 1866). Another general reported that states were not enforcing the criminal laws when blacks were victims. *Id.* at 425.

115. Report of the Joint Committee on Reconstruction, 39th Cong., XVII (1866).

116. The Black Codes are usefully described in Finkleman, *supra* note 110, at 45–47, and HYMAN & WIECEK, *supra* note 105, at 319–22. For a fuller account of the role of the Black Codes in Reconstruction, see ERIC FONER, RECONSTRUCTION: AMERICA'S UNFINISHED REVOLUTION, 1863–1877, at 198–216 (1988).

117. HYMAN & WIECEK, *supra* note 105, at 320 ("Some northern states enacted attenuated counterparts of the southern Black Codes in the same period, usually by prohibiting the ingress of blacks into the state, imposing Jim Crow in public facilities, or prohibiting blacks from voting.").

118. CHARLES FAIRMAN, 6 HISTORY OF THE SUPREME COURT OF THE UNITED STATES: RECONSTRUCTION AND REUNION, 1864–68, at 110 (1971). The Black Codes themselves are collected in Freedmen's Affairs, 39th Cong., 2nd Sess., Laws in Relation to Freedman 170–230 (Senate Exec. Doc. 6 1866).

119. Freedmen's Affairs, *supra* note 118, at 181–82.

120. *Id.* at 182.

121. FAIRMAN, *supra* note 118, at 116.

122. Freedmen's Affairs, *supra* note 118, at 192.

123. FAIRMAN, *supra* note 118, at 112–13.

124. Freedmen's Affairs, *supra* note 118, at 177.

125. *Id.* at 228–29.

126. *Id.* at 193.

127. *Id.*

128. *Id.* at 174.

129. *Id.* at 195.
130. FAIRMAN, *supra* note 118, at 115.
131. *Id.* at 110; *see also* HYMAN & WIECEK, *supra* note 105, at 334 (noting that "[t]he Black Codes called back to the colors, as it were, many old abolitionists," and that "a majority of the Republican Congressmen of 1866 were ready-on-the-mark to respond to the Black Code assault"). Eric Foner has written that "[n]ews of violence against the freedmen and the passage of the Black Codes aroused an indignation that spread far beyond Radical circles." FONER, *supra* note 116, at 225. Massachusetts Senator Henry Wilson wrote to Secretary of State Seward that the aim of the Thirty-Ninth Congress would not be black suffrage, but simply "the annulment of all laws against the freedmen and their full liberty." *Id.* at 227 (quoting Letter from Henry Wilson to William H. Seward, Nov. 20, 1865).

5   THE FOURTEENTH AMENDMENT

1. U.S. CONST. amend. XIV, § 1.
2. *Id.* at § 5.
3. *See* John Harrison, *Reconstructing the Privileges or Immunities Clause*, 101 YALE L.J. 1385, 1402 (1992).
4. Civil Rights Act of 1866, ch. 31, § 1, 14 Stat. 27 (1866) (emphases added).
5. CONG. GLOBE, 39th Cong., 1st Sess. 474 (1866).
6. *Id.*
7. *Id.*
8. CONG. GLOBE, 39th Cong., 1st Sess. app. 158 (remarks of Rep. Delano of Ohio).
9. CONG. GLOBE, 39th Cong., 1st Sess. 1121 (remarks of Rep. Rogers of New Jersey).
10. LILLIAN FOSTER, ANDREW JOHNSON, PRESIDENT OF THE UNITED STATES; HIS LIFE AND SPEECHES 269, 277–79 (1866).
11. KURT T. LASH, THE FOURTEENTH AMENDMENT AND THE PRIVILEGES AND IMMUNITIES OF AMERICAN CITIZENSHIP 137 & n.289 (2014).
12. HORACE EDGAR FLACK, THE ADOPTION OF THE FOURTEENTH AMENDMENT 40 (1908).
13. *Id.* at 46–54.
14. *See, e.g.*, JOSEPH B. JAMES, THE FRAMING OF THE FOURTEENTH AMENDMENT 50 (1956); WILLIAM E. NELSON, THE FOURTEENTH AMENDMENT: FROM POLITICAL PRINCIPLE TO JUDICIAL DOCTRINE 8 (1988); JACOBUS TENBROEK, EQUAL UNDER LAW 201–03 (1965); Philip Hamburger, *Privileges or Immunities*, 105 NW. U. L. REV. 61, 117 (2011).

15. CHRISTOPHER GREEN, EQUAL CITIZENSHIP, CIVIL RIGHTS, AND THE CONSTITUTION: THE ORIGINAL SENSE OF THE PRIVILEGES OR IMMUNITIES CLAUSE 44 (2015). For examples of statements connecting § 1 of the Fourteenth Amendment and the Civil Rights Act, see also JAMES, *supra* note 14, at 125–31 (1956).

16. JAMES, *supra* note 14, at 113.

17. FLACK, *supra* note 12, at 140–49.

18. *See, e.g.*, TENBROEK, *supra* note 14, at 225–26; FLACK, *supra* note 12, at 75; NELSON, *supra* note 14, at 55.

19. CONG. GLOBE, 39th Cong., 1st Sess. 2462 (1866) (Garfield). For other statements to this effect, see *id.* at 2459 (Stevens) (noting that the Fourteenth Amendment was necessary because the Civil Rights Act "is repealable by a majority" and that "the first time that the South with their copperhead allies obtain the command of Congress it will be repealed"); *id.* at 2465 (Thayer) (noting that the Fourteenth Amendment is necessary so that "the principle of the civil rights bill" will be "forever incorporated in the Constitution"); *id.* at 2498 (Broomall) (similar).

20. JAMES, *supra* note 14, at 29 (quoting CINCINNATI COMMERCIAL, Sept. 23, 1865).

21. H.R. 437, 39th Cong. (as reported by H. Comm. on the Judiciary, Apr. 2, 1866, Printers No. 116).

22. *Id.*

23. Hamburger, *supra* note 14, at 120.

24. H.R. 437, 39th Cong. (as reported by H. Comm. on the Judiciary, Apr. 2, 1866, Printers No. 116) §§ 2–4.

25. Hamburger, *supra* note 14, at 119–22. This seems odd, however, because if Congress had the power to enforce the fugitive slave clause – also in article IV of the Constitution – then surely it also had the power to pass legislation enforcing the comity clause. In any event, no further action was taken on the bill.

26. Second Freedmen's Bureau Act, ch. 200, 14 Stat. 173, 177 (1866) (enacted by veto override); Mark A. Graber, *The Second Freedmen's Bureau Bill's Constitution*, 94 TEX. L. REV. 1361, 1367 (2016).

27. Ch. 200, § 14, 14 Stat. 173, 176–77.

28. *Id.*

29. JAMES, *supra* note 14, at 50 (quoting CONG. GLOBE, 39th Cong., 1st Sess. 77 (1865)).

30. Graber, *supra* note 26, at 1372–90.

31. Christopher R. Green, *Loyal Denominatorism and the Fourteenth Amendment: Normative Defense and Implications*, 13 DUKE J. OF CON'L L. & PUB. POL'Y 168, 184–88 (2017).

32. Graber, *supra* note 26, at 1390–96.

33. Andrew Jackson, *Veto Message, in* POPULAR SERIES OF NATIONAL DOCUMENTS 4 (1866).

34. JAMES, *supra* note 14, at 84.
35. An Act to provide for the more efficient Government of the Rebel States, ch. 153, pmbl., 14 Stat. 428, 428 (Mar. 2, 1867).
36. *Id.* at § 3.
37. DAVID P. CURRIE, THE CONSTITUTION IN THE SUPREME COURT: THE FIRST HUNDRED YEARS, 1789–1888, at 300–06 (1990); *see also Mississippi v. Johnson,* 71 U.S. (4 Wall.) 475 (1866); *Georgia v. Stanton,* 73 U.S. (6 Wall.) 50 (1867); *Ex parte McCardle,* 74 U.S. (7 Wall.) 506 (1868); *Ex parte Yerger,* 75 U.S. (8 Wall.) 85 (1868).
38. CURRIE, *supra* note 37, at 303; U.S. CONST. art. IV, § 4.
39. 48 U.S. (7 How.) 1, 56 (1849).
40. CURRIE, *supra* note 37, at 303.
41. Andrew Johnson, President of the U.S., Veto of Reconstruction Bill (March 2, 1867), *in* EDWARD MCPHERSON, THE POLITICAL HISTORY OF THE UNITED STATES OF AMERICA DURING THE PERIOD OF RECONSTRUCTION (FROM APRIL 15, 1865, TO JULY 15, 1870), at 170 (3rd ed. 1880).
42. U.S. CONST. amend. XIV, § 1.
43. *Id.* at § 5.
44. We do not need to rely on any legislative history at all, but it is worth pointing out here that some of the more persuasive pieces of the legislative history support this reading of the privileges or immunities clause. On April 21, 1866, the proposal of Robert Dale Owen was introduced before the Joint Committee on Reconstruction. This was the initial proposal most closely aligned to the final version of the Fourteenth Amendment. It was on this day, as an amendment to this proposal, that Bingham added the exact words of what would become § 1 of the Fourteenth Amendment to the Owen proposal, as § 5. But earlier on that day, instead of adding these words as an entirely new section, Bingham had tried to amend the first section of the Owen proposal. That section provided: "No discrimination shall be made by any State, nor by the United States, as to civil rights of persons, because of race, color, or previous condition of servitude." To this Bingham sought to add "nor shall any state deny to any person within its jurisdiction the equal protection of the laws, nor take private property for public use without just compensation." *See* JAMES, *supra* note 14, at 100–04. This strongly suggests that, at that time, Bingham and others understood the work of the privileges or immunities clause to be antidiscriminatory in nature, notwithstanding Bingham's comments five years later in 1871 to the effect that he had intended to incorporate the Bill of Rights against the states.

   Additionally, Thaddeus Stevens was the leader of the Radical Republicans in the House, and he twice explained – before and after Bingham's language was drafted – that the purpose of the Amendment was to secure equality in state-defined civil rights. On December 5, 1865, Mr. Stevens moved for the first time a series of resolutions for amending the Constitution, each of which can be detected in some section of the final Amendment. The pertinent resolution for our purposes provided: "All national and state laws shall be equally applicable to every citizen, and no discrimination shall be made on account of race or color." CONG. GLOBE, 39th Cong., 1st Sess. 10 (1865).

Opening the debate in the House on the final form of the Amendment, Stevens, in reference to the first section, explained:

> [T]he Constitution limits only the action of Congress, and is not a limitation on the States. This Amendment supplies that defect, and allows Congress to correct the unjust legislation of the States, so far that the law which operates upon one man shall operate *equally* upon all. Whatever law punishes a white man for a crime shall punish the black man precisely in the same way and to the same degree. Whatever law protects the white man shall afford "equal" protection to the black man. Whatever means of redress is afforded to one shall be afforded to all. Whatever law allows the white man to testify in court shall allow the man of color to do the same.

Id. at 2459. To be sure, the equality with respect to punishment, redress, and testimony may all result from the requirement for equal protection of the laws – but it is nevertheless telling that the thrust of § 1 for Stevens was its requirement of equality.

Jacob Howard told the Senate that § 1 would abolish "class legislation" and the "injustice of subjecting one caste of persons to a code not applicable to another." *Id.* at 2766. In surveying the debates, William Nelson has written that "[t]he theme that section one of the Fourteenth Amendment did not direct states either to adopt or not to adopt particular legislation, but merely required that legislation treat all people equally, was reiterated again and again." NELSON, *supra* note 14, at 116.

This also appears to have been the understanding of the public. The *New York Times* editorialized after § 1 took shape: "All are willing to submit to the States [for ratification] the question of whether they will concede to Congress the power to prevent *unequal* State legislation touching the civil rights of citizens of the United States." May 31, 1866 (emphasis added), *quoted in* JAMES, *supra* note 14, at 145. And Bingham himself told the public in the campaign for ratification that § 1 was a "declaration that equal laws and equal and exact justice shall hereafter be secured within every State of this Union." THE CINCINNATI COMMERCIAL, SPEECHES OF THE CAMPAIGN OF 1866, IN THE STATES OF OHIO, INDIANA AND KENTUCKY 19 (1866).

45. *See, e.g.*, Garrett Epps, Democracy Reborn: The Fourteenth Amendment and the Fight for Equal Rights in Post-Civil War America 11 (2013) (noting that scholars have referred to the Fourteenth Amendment as "the second Constitution"); Infinite Hope and Finite Disappointment: The Story of the First Interpreters of the Fourteenth Amendment 11 (Elizabeth Reilly ed., 2013); Garrett Epps, *Second Founding: The Story of the Fourteenth Amendment*, 85 Or. L. Rev. 895 (2006); Rebecca E. Zeitlow, *The Rights of Citizenship: Two Framers, Two Amendments*, 11 U. Pa. J. Const. L. 1269, 1270 (2009). *See generally* Bruce Ackerman, We The People: Transformations 207 (1998)("As the Convention/Congress ended its special session in early spring, Republicans could look back on a period of creativity rivaling the Founding"); Nelson, *supra* note 14, at 44–46 (noting the "history-making character of Reconstruction" and the contemporary awareness of its historic character). *Cf.* Cong. Globe, 39th Cong., 1st Sess. 586 (1866) (Donnelly) ("[T]his is a new birth of the nation. The Constitution will hereafter be read by the light of the rebellion; by the light of the emancipation; by the light of that tremendous uprising of the intellect of the world going on everywhere around us."); Abraham Lincoln, Gettysburg Address (Nov. 19, 1863) ("It is rather for us to be here dedicated to the great task remaining before us . . . that this nation, under God, shall have a new birth of freedom . . . "). More recently, Eric Foner also published a book by the same primary title, although his book spans all three of the Reconstruction Amendments. *See* Eric Foner, The Second Founding: How The Civil War and Reconstruction Remade the Constitution (2019).

46. Abraham Lincoln, Gettysburg Address (Nov. 19, 1863).

6   PRIVILEGES, IMMUNITIES, AND INCORPORATION

1. Philip Hamburger, *Privileges or Immunities*, 105 Nw. U. L. Rev. 61, 61–62 (2011).
2. *Id.* at 104–15, 147.
3. Kurt T. Lash, The Fourteenth Amendment and the Privileges and Immunities of American Citizenship 47–66 (2014).
4. *Id.* at 65.
5. Akhil Reed Amar, The Bill of Rights: Creation and Reconstruction 163–80 (1998).
6. *Id.* at 180.
7. *Gibbons v. Ogden*, 22 U.S. (9 Wheat.) 1 (1824) (discussing a federal licensing scheme to engage in coasting trade); Act of July 22, 1790, 1 Stat. 137 (setting up licensing scheme for trading with native tribes).
8. 35 U.S.C. § 1 *et seq.*

9. LASH, *supra* note 3, at 48 (quoting Treaty of Purchase between the United States of America and the French Republic, art. III, U.S.–Fr., Apr. 30, 1803, 8 Stat. 200).
10. Civil Rights Act of 1866, ch. 31, § 1, 14 Stat. 27 (1866).
11. LILLIAN FOSTER, ANDREW JOHNSON, PRESIDENT OF THE UNITED STATES; HIS LIFE AND SPEECHES 266 (1866).
12. *Id.* at 267–68.
13. *Id.* at 268.
14. See Chapter 5.
15. CONG. GLOBE, 39th Cong., 1st Sess. 1757 (1866) (emphasis added).
16. CHRISTOPHER GREEN, EQUAL CITIZENSHIP, CIVIL RIGHTS, AND THE CONSTITUTION: THE ORIGINAL SENSE OF THE PRIVILEGES OR IMMUNITIES CLAUSE 45 (2015).
17. *Id.* at 46 (quoting THE CINCINNATI COMMERCIAL, SPEECHES OF THE CAMPAIGN OF 1866, at 14 (1866)).
18. *Address of the Colored Convention to the People of Alabama*, MONTGOMERY DAILY STATE SENTINEL, May 21, 1867 (emphasis in original), *in* MAJOR PROBLEMS IN THE CIVIL WAR AND RECONSTRUCTION: DOCUMENTS AND ESSAYS 394–95 (Michael Perman & Amy Murrell Taylor eds., 3rd ed., 2011).
19. HORACE EDGAR FLACK, THE ADOPTIONS OF THE FOURTEENTH AMENDMENT 153 (1908); *see also, e.g.,* AMAR, *supra* note 5, at 187–93 (describing Charles Fairman's critique that no one discussed incorporating the Bill of Rights during ratification, but arguing why we would not expect them to have done so). Amar claims that Michael Kent Curtis has shown that there was much more discussion about the Bill of Rights during ratification than Fairman let on. *Id.* at 197 (citing MICHAEL KENT CURTIS, NO STATE SHALL ABRIDGE: THE FOURTEENTH AMENDMENT AND THE BILL OF RIGHTS 131–53 (1986)). But, as far as I have been able to tell, none of Curtis's collected evidence demonstrates that anyone thought the Bill of Rights would apply against the states. What they show is that the *kinds* of privileges and immunities in the Bill of Rights – the right to speak, to bear arms, to assemble – are privileges and immunities within the meaning of the Civil Rights Act and the Fourteenth Amendment. But none suggests what an *abridgment* of those rights would be. As I shall explain shortly, it is entirely consistent with the equality reading of the clause to include state constitutional rights within its scope. All that means is that a state could not deny *blacks* the right to assemble or to bear arms when it allowed such privileges to whites.
20. Akhil Amar points to one or two such editorials. AMAR, *supra* note 5, at 187.
21. CONG. GLOBE, 39th Cong., 1st Sess. 2765–66 (1866).
22. To cite only the most recent example, *see* ERIC FONER, THE SECOND FOUNDING: HOW THE CIVIL WAR AND RECONSTRUCTION REMADE THE CONSTITUTION 75 (2019) ("John A. Bingham also explicitly stated that

privileges and immunities included the liberties enumerated in the Bill of Rights ... ").

23.   His full statement read:

> [I]n the event of the adoption of this amendment, if they conspire together to enact laws refusing equal protection to life, liberty, or property, the Congress is thereby vested with power to hold them to answer before the bar of the national courts for the violation of their oaths and of the rights of their fellowmen. Why should it not be so? That is the question. Why should it not be so? Is the bill of rights to stand in our Constitution hereafter, as in the past five years within eleven States, a mere dead letter? It is absolutely essential to the safety of the people that it should be enforced.

> CONG. GLOBE, 39th Cong., 1st Sess. 1090 (1866).

24.   *Id.* at 1089.

25.   *See* Gerard N. Magliocca, *The Bill of Rights as a Term of Art*, 92 NOTRE DAME L. REV. 231 (2016). Magliocca claims that the first use of the term in the Supreme Court as a reference to the first eight Amendments was 1897. *Id.* at 232 n.8 (citing *Robertson v. Baldwin*, 165 U.S. 275, 281 (1897)). All of this aside – or perhaps as these very statements show – Bingham may have been a muddled thinker. *See, e.g.*, RAOUL BERGER, THE FOURTEENTH AMENDMENT AND THE BILL OF RIGHTS 128–35 (1989); LEONARD W. LEVY, JUDGEMENTS: ESSAYS ON CONSTITUTIONAL HISTORY 77 (1972) (Bingham "was extremely confused and contradictory in his presentation"); Alexander M. Bickel, *The Original Understanding and the Segregation Decision*, 69 HARV. L. REV. 1, 25 (1955) (claiming that Bingham was "not normally distinguished for precision of thought and statement"); Wallace Mendelson, *Mr. Justice Black's Fourteenth Amendment*, 53 MINN. L. REV. 711, 716 (1969) (Bingham "used ringing rhetoric as substitute for rational analysis"). Kurt Lash discusses Bingham's various inconsistent statements and argues that the best explanation may be that he simply changed his mind – that he intended to refer to the privileges of national citizenship and incorrectly believed that invoking the privileges *and* immunities language of Article IV would do the trick. *See* LASH, *supra* note 3, at 70–73. This may be the case, but there is simply no *contemporaneous* evidence that Bingham changed his understanding in this way. The only evidence that Bingham initially believed that the comity clause language would protect the rights of national citizenship and later came to understand that the comity clause language referred only to privileges of *state* citizenship, and that he therefore changed the language to "citizens of the United States," are his statements in Congress in 1871. *See id.* at nn.10–18. This was, of course, five years after the debates in Congress and three years

after ratification. There is no evidence that anyone understood Bingham to be changing his mind in this way in 1866.

26. Cong. Globe, 42d Cong., 1st Sess. 84 app. (1871) (statement of Rep. Bingham).

27. Levy, *supra* note 26, at 77.

28. For reliance on Bingham's 1871 statement in the literature, *see, e.g.,* Akhil Reed Amar, *The Bill of Rights and the Fourteenth Amendment,* 101 Yale L.J. 1193, 1219 (1992).

29. The text of the Fourteenth Amendment may even specifically account for the state-defined privileges of U.S. citizens. The privileges or immunities clause appears after the sentence declaring that "[a]ll persons born or naturalized in the United States and subject to the jurisdiction thereof, are citizens of the United States and of the State wherein they reside." This clause declares these individuals to be citizens *both* of the United States *and* of the "State wherein they reside." As John Harrison has explained, the privileges or immunities of this *group of individuals* – these citizens of the United States – include *also* their privileges and immunities *as citizens of the respective states.* John Harrison, *Reconstructing the Privileges or Immunities Clause,* 101 Yale L. J. 1385, 1414–15 (1992). In any event, as John Harrison has observed, the whole point of the clause was to *make* equality in state-defined privileges and immunities itself a privilege of national citizenship. The Amendment, Harrison explains, does not "divide" state and national citizenship, but rather "staples them together." *Id.* at 1415.

30. Amar, *supra* note 29, at 1222.

31. Ala. Const. of 1868, art. I, § 2.

32. Ark. Const. of 1868, art. I, § 3.

33. La. Const. of 1868, tit. I, art. 2.

34. S.C. Const. of 1868, art. I, § 39.

35. Tex. Const. of 1869, art. I, § 21.

36. An Act to protect all citizens in their civil and legal rights, ch. 114, 18 Stat. 335, 336 (1875).

37. Michael W. McConnell, *Originalism and the Desegregation Decisions,* 81 Va. L. Rev. 947, 1080 (1995).

38. Christopher Green collects numerous statements to this effect. Green, *supra* note 16, at 164–202 (Appendix D).

39. As Christopher Green concludes, "[t]he sheer number of these pieces of evidence" over the course of the debates over the 1875 Civil Rights Act – "both from framers of the Fourteenth Amendment, republished information from members of the public, and other Congressmen who, if not framers, were obviously also involved in public life in 1866" – goes a long way toward convincingly establishing the antidiscrimination reading of the clause. According to this reading, "the Privileges or Immunities Clause bans second-class citizenship – in the paradigm case, giving

white citizens one set of privileges and black citizens a different set." *Id.* at 97.

40. Amar, *supra* note 29, at 1203–12.

41. 32 U.S. (7 Pet.) 243 (1833).

42. Amar, *supra* note 29, at 1209; *see also* CURTIS, *supra* note 17, at 22–25.

43. CURTIS, *supra* note 18, at 15.

44. Randy E. Barnett, *Whence Comes Section One? The Abolitionist Origins of the Fourteenth Amendment,* 3 J. OF LEGAL ANALYSIS 165, 249–50 (2011).

45. *Id.* at 174–246.

46. *See, e.g., id.* at 193–94, 213, 219, 254.

47. *Id.* at 254.

48. *Id.* at 224–27. Barnett himself recognizes that Tiffany was "[u]nlike previous writers" in his analysis of the privileges and immunities clause of Article IV. *Id.* at 226.

49. Amar, *supra* note 29, at 1203–05.

50. *Id.*

51. *Id.* at 1210–11 (citing *Nunn v. Georgia,* 1 Ga. 243 (1846); *Campbell v. State,* 11 Ga. 353 (1852)). This is the same evidence on which Michael Kent Curtis relies. *See* CURTIS, *supra* note 18, at 22–25.

52. *Nunn,* 1 Ga. at 9–11; Alice Marie Beard, *Resistance by Inferior Courts to Supreme Court's Second Amendment Decisions,* 81 TENN. L. REV. 673, 691–92 (2014).

53. Jason Mazzone, *The Bill of Rights in the Early State Courts,* 92 MINN. L. REV. 1, 32–55 (2007). Amar understands this too and explains that many of the state-level decisions were driven by the "declaratory" theory of rights. Amar, *supra* note 29, at 1205–12.

54. *Id.* at 35–37 (describing such cases in the Fourth Amendment context).

55. CURTIS, *supra* note 18, at 31–32.

56. Perhaps the Republicans really did want to federalize First Amendment rights notwithstanding equivalent state provisions, believing that doing so would put those rights into better hands. One has reason to doubt Congress would have had such faith in the federal courts after *Dred Scott v. Sandford,* 60 U.S. (19 How.) 393 (1857).

57. William Nelson has similarly observed that most American states provided the same protections as those found in the federal Bill of Rights, and so Howard's and Bingham's statements about the Bill of Rights could easily have been referring to state constitutional equivalents. Thus "a state would be free to disregard entirely a provision of the Bill of Rights," but could not discriminate in providing a right. WILLIAM E. NELSON, THE FOURTEENTH AMENDMENT: FROM POLITICAL PRINCIPLE TO JUDICIAL DOCTRINE 118–19 (1988).

58. Randy E. Barnett, *After All These Years, Lochner Was Not Crazy – It Was Good,* 16 GEO. J.L. & PUB. POL'Y 437, 442 (2018); Randy E. Barnett & Evan

D. Bernick, *The Privileges or Immunities Clause, Abridged: A Critique of Kurt Lash on the Fourteenth Amendment*, 95 NOTRE DAME L. REV. 499, 499–503 (2019).

59.   6 F. Cas. 546 (C.C.E.D. Pa. 1825).
60.   *See* Barnett, *supra* note 59, at 440–41; Barnett & Bernick, *supra* note 59, at 500.
61.   *Corfield*, 6 F. Cas. at 551–52.
62.   Barnett, *supra* note 59, at 442–43.
63.   Harrison, *supra* note 30, at 1465–66.
64.   U.S. CONST., amend. XIV, § 2.
65.   Harrison, *supra* note 30, at 1421.
66.   *Id.* Christopher Green agrees that usage at the time implied a denial of equality. GREEN, *supra* note 16, at 84–86.
67.   U.S. CONST., amend. I.
68.   *See Rosenberger v. Rector and Visitors of Univ. of Va.*, 515 U.S. 819, 829 (1995) ("When the government targets not subject matter, but particular views taken by speakers on a subject, the violation of the First Amendment is all the more blatant. Viewpoint discrimination is thus an egregious form of content discrimination. The government must abstain from regulating speech when the specific motivating ideology or the opinion or perspective of the speaker is the rationale for the restriction."); *Lamb's Chapel v. Ctr. Moriches Union Free Sch. Dist.*, 508 U.S. 384, 384–85 (1993); *Boos v. Barry*, 485 U.S. 312, 321 (1988).

7   THE PAST AND FUTURE OF THE FOURTEENTH AMENDMENT

1.   83 U.S. 36 (1872).
2.   *Id.* at 82.
3.   163 U.S. 537, 555 (1896).
4.   *United States v. Cruikshank*, 92 U.S. 542 (1876).
5.   198 U.S. 45 (1905).
6.   347 U.S. 483, 495 (1954).
7.   347 U.S. 497, 500 (1954).
8.   *See Williamson v. Lee Optical of Oklahoma Inc.*, 348 U.S. 483 (1955); *United States v. Carolene Products Co.*, 304 U.S. 144 (1938).
9.   *Gitlow v. New York*, 268 U.S. 652 (1925) (applying the First Amendment against the states).
10.   381 U.S. 479 (1965).
11.   539 U.S. 558 (2003).
12.   135 S. Ct. 2584 (2015).
13.   92 U.S. 542 (1876).
14.   109 U.S. 3 (1883).

15. 377 U.S. 533 (1964).
16. Civil Rights Act of 1875, ch. 114, 18 Stat. 335, 336 (Mar. 1, 1875).
17. *Civil Rights Cases*, 109 U.S. at 11.
18. *Id.*
19. *Id.* at 19.
20. *Id.* at 24.
21. 163 U.S. 537 (1896).
22. *Civil Rights Cases*, 109 U.S. at 37–41, 58 (Harlan, J., dissenting).
23. *Cruikshank*, 92 U.S. at 552.
24. 379 U.S. 241, 261–62 (1964).
25. *Civil Rights Cases*, 109 U.S. at 37–38 (Harlan, J., dissenting).
26. *Id.* at 41.
27. *Id.* at 58.
28. *Markham v. Brown*, 8 N.H. 523, 528 (1837).
29. BOUVIER'S LAW DICTIONARY 285 (1843).
30. JAMES KENT, 2 COMMENTARIES ON AMERICAN LAW 599 (William M. Lacy ed., 1889).
31. *Brown*, 347 U.S. at 489 ("Reargument was largely devoted to the circumstances surrounding the adoption of the Fourteenth Amendment in 1868. It covered exhaustively consideration of the Amendment in Congress, ratification by the states, then-existing practices in racial segregation, and the views of proponents and opponents of the Amendment. This discussion and our own investigation convince us that, although these sources cast some light, it is not enough to resolve the problem with which we are faced. At best, they are inconclusive.").
32. *Id.* at 494.
33. Steven G. Calabresi & Michael W. Perl, *Originalism and Brown v. Board of Education*, 2014 MICH. ST. L. REV. 429.
34. *See* ILAN WURMAN, A DEBT AGAINST THE LIVING: AN INTRODUCTION TO ORIGINALISM 39, 113–14 (2017) (explaining the sense–reference distinction).
35. CONG. GLOBE, 39th Cong., 1st Sess. 1117 (1866).
36. *Id.* (quoting BOUVIER'S LAW DICTIONARY).
37. *See* Chapter 3.
38. IND. CONST. of 1851, art. I § 23.
39. Michael W. McConnell, *Originalism and the Desegregation Decisions*, 81 VA. L. REV. 947, 1055–57 (1995).
40. 6 F. Cas. 546, 552 (C.C.E.D. Pa. 1825).
41. *Bolling*, 347 U.S. at 500.
42. I do not mean to suggest that the federal government must create federal courts to hear such claims; state courts can hear them, consistent with the "Madisonian Compromise." Martin H. Redish & Curtis E. Woods, *Congressional Power to Control the Jurisdiction of Lower Federal Courts: A Critical Review and a New Synthesis*, 124 U. PA. L. REV. 45, 52–56

(1975). This compromise is rooted in the text of the Constitution, which states that "[t]he judicial Power of the United States shall be vested in one supreme Court, and in such inferior Courts as the Congress *may* from time to time ordain and establish." U.S. CONST. art. III, § 1 (emphasis added).

43. As Akhil Amar has explained, historically, Fourth Amendment claims would be resolved in state common-law actions against federal officers. AKHIL AMAR, THE BILL OF RIGHTS: CREATION AND RECONSTRUCTION 64–77 (1998).

44. 5 U.S. (1 Cranch) 137, 163 (1803).

45. In the sixth of the Kentucky Resolutions protesting the Alien and Sedition Acts of 1798, Jefferson wrote that because the Alien Friends Act purported to authorize the president to remove a person out of the United States "who is under the protection of the Law, on his own suspicion, without accusation, without jury, without public trial, without confrontation of the witnesses against him, without having witnesses in his favour, without defence, without counsel," that law was contrary to both the Fifth and Sixth Amendments. Resolutions Adopted by the Kentucky General Assembly, *in* 30 THE PAPERS OF THOMAS JEFFERSON, 1 JANUARY 1798 TO 31 JANUARY 1799, at 552 (2003).

46. Abolitionists complained that the Fugitive Slave Act of 1793, which led to the kidnapping of many free blacks in the border and Northern states on the barest of "legal" process, was in violation of the federal due process of law clause. JACOBUS TENBROEK, EQUAL UNDER LAW 61–65 (1965); *see also* HAROLD M. HYMAN & WILLIAM M. WIECEK, EQUAL JUSTICE UNDER LAW: CONSTITUTIONAL DEVELOPMENT, 1836–1875, at 107 (1982). Thus some Northern states insisted on supplementing the federal fugitive slave law with additional procedures as a matter of state law. The abolitionist William Goodell connected the lack of process with the denial of protection in an 1834 appeal to the people of New York against mob rule against the abolitionists:

> Neighbor, suppose someone hated you so violently that he wished to have you mobbed, and should get up a false report about you, pretending that you had done this thing and that thing and the other, that you never even thought of – and suppose by this means, one hundred men should be persuaded to surround your house, and pelt it with stones, and drag out your furniture and burn it, without once stopping to find out whether or no the man who accused you could prove the truth of his charges against you: what would you think of it and what kind of a "land of liberty" would you think you lived in, where your enemies had only to accuse you in order to get you punished – whether guilty or not – whether the offense charged upon you were any breach of the law or not – and all this without any court, or judge,

or jury! And yet, this is the way in which abolitionists have been treated.

TENBROEK, *supra*, at 120 (quoting William Goodell, An Appeal in Behalf of the American Anti-Slavery Society Addressed to the People of the City of New York, Aug. 1834); *see also id.* at 65 ("The equal protection to all which is the assurance of effectual protection to any was to be provided, and the practice of kidnapping free Negroes and selling them into slavery was to be reduced by supplying to the alleged fugitive the jury trial of the issue of his slavery guaranteed by the due process clause. So, once again, the ideas of equal protection and due process of law, together with man's natural and inalienable rights, are found in combination, supplementing and amplifying each other, providing between them the source and duty of affirmative authority and prescribing the character of its exercise, serving in the hands of the abolitionists the cause of free men marked out by the community for separate treatment."). "From the very beginning of its abolitionist usage," tenBroek writes, "due process was viewed not merely as a restraint on governmental power but as an obligation imposed upon government to supply protection against private action. Not to supply such protection was regarded as a denial or deprivation of due process of law." *Id.* at 121.

47. In *Ex parte Milligan*, 71 U.S. (4 Wall.) 2 (1866), the Court held that a civilian could not be tried by military courts in the northern parts of the Union where the ordinary courts had been open during the Civil War. Milligan's counsel argued that "political offenders are precisely the class of persons who most need the protection of a court and jury," and observed that "all who reside inside of our own territory are to be treated as under the protection of the law. If they help the enemy they are criminals, but they cannot be punished without legal conviction." *Id.* at 81. Here, Milligan's attorney explicitly connected protection and process. The Supreme Court agreed:

> [I]t is the birthright of every American citizen when charged with crime, to be tried and punished according to law. The power of punishment is, alone through the means which the laws have provided for that purpose, and if they are ineffectual, there is an immunity from punishment . . . By the protection of the law human rights are secured; withdraw that protection, and they are at the mercy of wicked rulers, or the clamor of an excited people.
> *Id.* at 119.

48. In terms of the protective function of the law, that, too, was supplied by the Constitution in the provision that the laws must be faithfully executed. U.S. CONST. art. II, § 3.

49. Ryan C. Williams, *Originalism and the Other Desegregation Decision*, 99 VA. L. REV. 493 (2013).

50. 3 JOSEPH STORY, COMMENTARIES ON THE CONSTITUTION OF THE UNITED STATES § 1800, 674–75 (1833) (emphasis added).

51. 2 JAMES KENT, COMMENTARIES ON AMERICAN LAW 61 (1827) (emphasis added).

52. COMM. ON COMMERCE, 27TH CONG., REP. ON FREE COLORED SEAMEN – MAJORITY AND MINORITY REPS. 3–4 (Comm. Print. 1843).

53. This raises the question of whether the privileges or immunities clause is superfluous. If citizenship required equality of rights, then why did the framers of the Amendment need to specify that the privileges and immunities of citizens could not be abridged? The answer may be as simple as the fact that many states had been ignoring the proposition that citizenship required equality, and therefore a specific injunction toward the states was still necessary.

54. GARY LAWSON & GUY SEIDMAN, "A GREAT POWER OF ATTORNEY": UNDERSTANDING THE FIDUCIARY CONSTITUTION 151–71 (2017).

55. *Lochner*, 198 U.S at 53.

56. 139 S. Ct. 2484, 2508 (2019).

57. *Id.* at 2514 (Kagan, E., dissenting).

58. 377 U.S. at 586–87.

59. Those are the Amendments providing that the right to vote shall not be abridged on the basis of color or sex. U.S. CONST. amends. XIV, XIX.

60. For the rights protected today by state constitutions, see Steven Gow Calabresi et al., *Individual Rights under State Constitutions in 2018: What Rights Are Deeply Rooted in a Modern-Day Consensus of States?*, 94 NOTRE DAME L. REV. 49 (2018).

61. 558 U.S. 310 (2010).

62. So called after *Miranda v. Arizona*, 384 U.S. 436 (1966).

63. 59 U.S. (18 How.) 272, 277 (1856).

64. WURMAN, *supra* note 36, at 43–44.

65. William Baude, *Constitutional Liquidation*, 71 STAN. L. REV. 1 (2019).

66. THE FEDERALIST No. 37, at 223–25 (James Madison) (Clinton Rossiter ed., 1961); *see also* Caleb Nelson, *Originalism and Interpretive Conventions*, 70 U. CHI. L. REV. 519, 525–36 (2003).

67. 521 U.S. 507 (1997).

68. 570 U.S. 529 (2013).

69. 494 U.S. 872 (1990).

70. For arguments along these lines, *see* Michael W. McConnell, *Institutions and Interpretation: A Critique of City of Boerne v. Flores*, 111 HARV. L. REV. 153 (1997).

INDEX

Made in the USA
Las Vegas, NV
01 October 2022

56328762R00115